HARVESTING GOLD:

THOMAS EDISON'S EXPERIMENT TO RE-INVENT AMERICAN MONEY

By David L. Hammes

First edition, March 2012

ISBN: 978-0-9850667-03

Edited, designed, produced, and distributed by
Richard Mahler Publications
P.O. Box 1055
Silver City, NM 88062
575.534.4841
www.richardmahler.com

For Kathy.

When we met time stood still and all was possible.

TABLE OF CONTENTS

ACKNOWLEDGMENTS

The idea that this material might be a book people wished to read goes back to a summertime suggestion from my cousin, Mrs. Eileen Strom Johnson, while we were in her fragrant garden in Minneapolis, Minnesota. At that time, interest from an audience wider than a few economists dealing in doctrinal issues, had not occurred to me. This book got started on lemonade, 'Minnesota Nice' and Eileen's ability to 'hear' a story where there was only inchoate rambling.

The reason there was any 'Edison material' in my hands at all goes back to 1999 and a classroom question about the structure of the Federal Reserve System from Ms. Jessica Schweig. That question led me by invitation to the Federal Reserve's library and archives in the Eccles building in Washington, D.C., leading in July of 2001 to Henry Parker Willis and his curt exchanges with Thomas Edison housed at Columbia University's Willis Collection. It seems as straightforward as a three-cushion shot in billiards with twists, turns, and many intervening years.

Through the years from 2001, Douglas T. Wills, of the University of Washington-Tacoma, and I pursued the Edison story producing academic papers from material Doug found in the Edison Archives at the Thomas Edison National Historical Park in late 2001. These papers are cited in this book.

Then we both waited expectantly through the decade for the Park to re-open following extensive renovation, finally making a joint research trip there in late September 2009 just prior to its public re-opening. At that time, Doug photographed nearly the entire Banking collection and put the material into electronic form.

Beyond the published papers, many people have been encouraging along the way. Led by my aunt (Eileen's mother), Mrs. Pauline Strom and her genial: "How's the book going?", friends and family were politely curious just often enough to remind me they expected to read something rather than listen to me recite letters from Edison's correspondents.

Delightful conversations over lunch with Professor Mark Panek, Department of English, University of Hawaii-Hilo, in mid-2011 helped me organize my thoughts. Mark's proven experience at writing books people wish to keep reading is an inspiration as is his willingness to share ideas and techniques.

Many people have read earlier, partial or full, versions of this manuscript and have generously given very helpful comments. I have gratefully incorporated most of them, ignoring others at my peril. My wife, Kathy Hammes, Mrs. Pauline Strom, Professors Robert Stack and Jerry Calton, Dr. Stanley Fortuna, Jr., Dr. William Gibson, Dr. Constance Chiba, Mr. Richard Mahler, my former students Robin Aguiar-

Hicks and Nathan Gaddis, and Ms. Karen Sloat-Olsen…all made penetrating and enlightening comments and suggestions on a full or near-full version that led to a much improved and compelling narrative. Readers and I owe them a very great debt of gratitude.

Mark and Steven Hammes, Laureè Enos, David and Liz Chiba, Mark, Jane and David Carson, Judith Branch, and Laura Marler all read portions of earlier versions. Their comments and encouragements were no less helpful in getting me through challenging expositional traverses. As with those named above, I am grateful for the fresh eyes and helpful comments they devoted to this project.

Early on I was fortunate to have Ms. Laura Marler as a volunteer research assistant. Her enthusiasm for the project preceded my ability to direct her time productively, but she was able to make many helpful 'finds' that propel and inform the story.

None of what follows could have happened without the expert help and patient assistance of Mr. Leonard DeGraaf, Archivist, of the Thomas Edison National Historical Park, National Park Service, U.S. Department of the Interior. Along with Ms. Karen Sloat-Olsen, the Park's Chief of Interpretation and Education, Leonard fielded many anxious e-mails and phone calls over the 2002-2009 period while the Park was closed to the public.

Once at the site, Leonard efficiently found material, made suggestions, and made every effort to accommodate our requests. As well, he gave us tours of the site and helped us delve more deeply into the environment with which Thomas Edison surrounded himself.

The voluminous letters and correspondence in the Park's collection is used with the following caveat from Mr. DeGraaf (private correspondence, January 4, 2012): "We don't own the rights to any of the documents or photos in the Edison archives, so we can neither deny nor grant publication permission. For photographs we request a source credit. The preferred credit is U.S. Dept. of the Interior, National Park Service, Thomas Edison National Historical Park. For documents, anything created by Edison, the Edison company or Edison employees passed into the public domain when the company donated the collection to the U.S. govt. For documents or letters received by Edison, the NPS owns the physical letter, but not the rights to the contents. You would need to follow the Library of Congress guidelines to determine the copyright status of those works. This would apply to documents you would want to reproduce entirely."

For full and partial funding of those research trips in 2001 and 2009, I thank the College of Business and Economics, University of Hawaii at Hilo. The College has — and my colleagues have always — been extremely tolerant of my musings, sometimes rantings, about money, Edison, and I'm sure the almost mythical-sounding "Archives in West Orange".

In addition to reading a previous draft, Mr. Richard Mahler has expertly handled the 'production side' of getting this book out to the public. I know nothing and wish to know even less, about what needs to happen to the words I write to get them before the public. Richard is an 'author's author'. The writer of a dozen published books, he actually enjoys knowing what happens to the words between their writing and appearing on the page. Without someone like Richard willing to do that, and other hard work, these words would lie stillborn in cloud storage.

Though the world has hurried on, the light bulb is now a compact fluorescent or LED; the phonograph is an iPod, movies are streaming videos, the name "Edison" still evokes magic, inspiration, and invention. When I buttonhole someone and start my monologue their glazing eyes focus sharply and their attention is full when I say his magic name. If I forgot a pithy comment or helpful suggestion from one of these listeners or readers, I apologize to anyone left unacknowledged. Most projects are a collective endeavor and one forgets to note every comment or encouraging word. Through the years I have received many of both.

INTRODUCTION

My introduction to Thomas Edison's monetary experimenting started on a warm July day in 2001 in the Rare Book and Manuscript Library at Columbia University. Doug Wills and I were going through the Henry Willis Parker collection in hopes of writing a biography of one of America's influential — but, we thought, under-known and under-appreciated — early twentieth-century economists. While reading through the files we happened upon a copy of a February 1922 letter from Willis to Thomas Edison declining to participate in his survey. What? Edison? Survey? Someone — Henry Parker Willis — saying "No," and saying it rather rudely? What was this all about?

Imagine if Bill Gates and Steve Jobs (before his untimely passing) — Edison, for his time, is bigger than both of them — tweeted you asking for your opinion on money and banking. How would you respond? How would today's experts respond? If Edison sent a letter to cranky Willis, maybe he sent it to other economists? Obviously, being economists, we wanted to race down this path and see where it led. Perhaps the answers, if there were any, would shed light on monetary thought in the 1920s. Maybe the economists would write something in confidence to Edison that they had not put in public print. Maybe we could write an academic article or two out of this trip.

Thanks to Doug's industry, more information from other economists and bankers was found in the archives at the Thomas Edison National Historic Park (TENHP) in West Orange, NJ, and we ultimately squeezed four papers out of that research.

Nobel-winning economist Milton Friedman's generous comment on one of our drafts (Hammes-Wills, 2006) — "Thank you for sending me a copy of your fascinating paper on Edison's monetary proposal. It is fascinating that such intelligent, inventive minds as Edison's can be so misguided on matters of economic policy...He was right about one thing: the gold standard did not make any more sense except for the fact that it had been widely adopted and it was much easier to store one commodity than many." (Private message, May 19, 2005) — brought up more issues and gave me reason to think a wide variety of readers might enjoy this episode in Edison's life.

What Doug found initially, and what we both saw eight years later in the fall of 2009, was that there are literally hundreds of pages to and from Edison on this topic.[1] These are letters to and from many people, some well known, most obscure. Edison was no stranger to the halls of Congress and government offices and agencies, he was no

[1] Why eight years' (2001 to 2009) delay? The TENHP was closed for renovation. It is open now.

stranger to Wall Street, nor was he a stranger to the common man, the farmer. Maybe there was more to the Edison-money story in this data 'dump'?

This book is my answer. Edison was convinced that gold as a foundation for money was wasteful, dangerous, and could not persist. In his view — contra the experts of his day — he was absolutely correct. Today, gold does not back our money. Yet, political debates are fueled by calls for a return to gold. Central banks buy gold. Gold's price rises and falls quickly, driven by monetary factors having little or nothing to do with its value as a decorative and industrial commodity. By buying gold, are central banks being prudent stewards or implicitly betting against their own currencies?

Also clear is that Edison was making a plan for the nation's monetary future and he was willing to wait. He had the patience borne of years of experimenting, waiting for patterns to emerge, and then moving one step forward.

From Edison's writing, it is evident that he was confident enough that, if policy makers of the 1920s were unreceptive, future policy makers might use his work. He expected it. What's more ironic, when looked at through Edison-colored lenses, current Federal Reserve policy, trail-bossed by Ben Bernanke, does seem to have been lifted out of Edison's guidebook. Wouldn't that amuse the old inventor!

Consider our current monetary system as you read this. Are there any parallels? Can we learn anything from the early 1920s? Should we heed George Santayana's oft-repeated caution: "Those who cannot remember the past are condemned to repeat it."

Was Edison a famous inventor thinking that his genius in one area was easily transferable? Did his high self-assessment see him knocking about unfamiliar territory proposing ultimately kooky solutions to real problems? Did he have anything to add or was his effort misdirection adding only confusion to an already tumultuous time and economic situation?

As you open your networking site, if there is a message from Bill Gates or the next Steve Jobs asking for your opinion on their monetary plan, how will *you* respond?

Thomas Alva Edison, 1915.

Courtesy of the University of Texas Libraries,
The University of Texas at Austin.

CHAPTER 1: THE FINANCIAL MELTDOWN

"Confidence and the debt-paying and purchasing power have practically been destroyed. Bankruptcies, suicides and the enormous increase in insanity are proof positive of the seriousness of the situation…the suffering of the people is simply appalling."(a)

"The wheat farmer who placed a mortgage on his land to purchase supplies and hired labor to plant his crop, must now pay with two bushels of wheat what he could have then bought with one, and other producer's suffer in like manner."(b)

"…thousands of unheralded suicides, and untold anguish, this vile New York crowd, because of the exaggerated market swings, and the attending influences of CALL on TIME money, bring about our ever repeating Insane Economic Cycles…with the result that business is always too fast or too slow, and the crashes that come with strangulated and frozen credits paralyze the solid world of commerce, throwing millions of our honest, sturdy toilers out of employment."(c)[2]

When the economic bubble burst, collapse struck quickly leaving bitter losers littered across the United States. Unemployment skyrocketed and prices fell precipitously. Farmers and 'Main Streeters' blamed Wall Street speculators and 'Shylock loan men' for collapsed markets and lost livelihoods. Defaulters ran away from debts imperiling more and more banks and hobbling any chance of rapid recovery. The paralyzed Federal government deepened the economic freeze by dramatically reducing scheduled spending, started sales of government assets to reduce debt levels, while giving no clear guidance on future spending or tax policies.

In Europe, it was worse. Entire countries threatened defaults on their domestic and international loan obligations. Everywhere one looked there was global political and economic instability. Currencies were in crisis. International conferences to re-organize the financial and political world worsened the instability breaking down in accusations, blame-finding, and finger pointing.

Moving in to the presidential election cycle in the U.S., the unpopular second-term president waited expectantly for a call from his party's convention for a run at a third consecutive term. That did not happen. The new president would be inheriting a country riven by the recent war, an economy in freefall, and bleak prospects. Placed against the national and international backdrop of financial and political up-

---

[2] (a) J.S. Wannamaker, South Carolina cotton grower and first president of the American Cotton Association, to Thomas Edison, April 29, 1922.
(b) I. Ludlow, Ludlow Syndicate, New York City, to Edison, April 17, 1922;
(c) M.B. Herman, St. Paul, MN, to Edison, September 10, 1922. All in the Banking, 1922, collection housed at the Thomas Edison National Historic Park, West Orange, New Jersey.

heaval, the candidate's platforms would signal to the country and the world the way ahead.

'Return to Normalcy', Warren Harding's 1920 campaign slogan, was ironically stark. What was 'normal' in a world of new countries, shifting borders, collapsing economies, new alliances, and war-driven high technology change? Yet, the slogan, harkening back to the simpler and more prosperous pre-war time, resonated with the weary electorate. Harding won an overwhelming victory.

In global politics, the U.S. spurned the League of Nations. Yet, due to its demonstrated ability to rapidly mount, mobilize, and deliver military might across vast distance, it could no longer maintain its pre-war 'isolationist' stance. Even if political isolationism was the hope of the war-weary people and Congress, like a large body in space, the U.S. would exert influence at-a-distance on countries around the world.

What had been 'normal'? The frame of reference was the rising standards of living world-wide between the mid-1870s to World War One. Global trade grew dramatically supported by an inter-locked world financial system based on the gold standard. The gold standard provided stability and predictable purchasing power by fixing currency values in terms of gold, the world's most widely recognized and accepted precious metal, and through gold, in terms of each other.

The gold standard acted as an anchor for international currencies, reducing exchange uncertainty, expanding trade. If prices rose faster in one country relative to another, the gold standard mechanism automatically set in motion re-balancing financial flows maintaining international values. As we see in more detail later, this mechanism worked automatically reducing the mischief of political influence in the international trade environment. Through improved transportation and the solid financial foundation, international trade and incomes grew rapidly. So rapidly that many observers hoped ruinous wars between countries would become obsolete due to the unacceptably large economic losses they imposed on belligerents.

After the devastating World War One, people questioned, 'Can national and international trade rebound?' Contrary to contemporary media presentations of the 1920s, the immediate post-war years were grim and gritty in most countries, including the U.S. 'Bubbles' and popping bubbles, rapidly inflating and deflating prices, the trade-destroying violent swings in currency values, unemployment, a severely depressed farm sector, these problems needed a permanent solution. The gold standard had seemingly failed the world.

Waiting to take on the challenge were the nation's bank, the Federal Reserve System, Congress, academics, and, surprisingly, the head of the country's first multimedia, innovative, entertainment conglomerate, the famous inventor, Thomas A. Edison.

Edison, at the time arguably the most identifiable person in the world, was famous for inventions and innovation. Dubbed 'The Wizard of Menlo Park,' he garnered more than one thousand patents and international honors for inventing or improving the hardware and the software of telegraphy, stock tickers, electric light, electricity systems, large storage batteries, the telephone, fluoroscopy, motion pictures, and phonographs. As one of the inspirations behind the popular "Tom Swift" books, he defined the word *genius* worldwide.

His every utterance and opinion was chronicled in the newspapers of the day. On the anniversaries of his birthday newsmen asked for his reflections and opinions and these stories were printed widely. Changes or proposals in government policies were typically fodder for his comment. His forecasts of coming technological changes were widely sought. If he thought the equivalent of a new iPad or iPhone was about to be launched people around the world wanted to know, as did the financial markets.

At the end of World War One he was in his early seventies, working daily at his laboratory and manufacturing complex in West Orange, New Jersey, as he would almost until his death in 1931. Living nearby at "Glenmont", bought as a wedding present for his second wife, his long, disciplined, life of invention, innovation, refinement, and production brought him into contact, sometimes conflict, with most of the well known people of several generations. From Jay Gould to J.P. Morgan, he learned how the financial system might be used to fund business activity. He often felt as if others did better than he did from his inventions. He was driven to tinker, to puzzle, to use theory and evidence and perspiration to find answers. Remember, it was Edison who said: "Genius is one percent inspiration and ninety-nine percent perspiration."

His friends included other 'big' names of his day, like the carmaker, Henry Ford. He first met Ford in 1896 when Ford, then thirty-two years old, was experimenting with an internal combustion engine. Ironically, given his work on batteries, Edison gave Ford emphatic support for his gas-powered idea. The younger Ford idolized Edison and the two were close friends from the 1900s onward.

Edison was feted internationally, meeting kings, monarchs, presidents, and was considered a valuable sounding-board and wise appraiser of ideas and people. He was self-made, started from humble beginnings, outworked others, imbued with a sharp-eye and tongue, he had a pithy aphorism for almost every occasion. Average people felt they understood him and they trusted him. As a parent, three children with his first wife, and three with Mina, his second wife, he was down-to-earth, most often absent, away in the lab, but with twinkles-in-his-eyes, creating little machines, explosives, and other divertissements for the younger children.

Because his inventions were omnipresent in their daily lives, people in the darkest hours after World War One still looked to him to provide more solutions and more products to ease their lives. In the financial turmoil of the post war period, at the urging of his friend Ford, he purposely turned his inventive mind from product development to the task of engineering a currency of permanently stable purchasing power — a dollar that would stay a dollar! — for the U.S. His efforts would catch the imagination and hopes of many, the respect and scorn of some, and his thoughts and theory would be splashed across the pages of the nation's newspapers.

Far from being moldy relics of a simpler, more rustic time, Edison's monetary ideas are echoing through the halls of today's central banks.

CHAPTER 2: NO BOMBS, BUT SEVERE ECONOMIC DEVASTATION

If there is one thing everyone 'knows' about the ending of World War One in November 1918 it is that it launched a decade of rapid social and economic advance in the United States. The popular view has soldiers coming back from 'over there' marching straight into the *Roaring* Twenties, refusing life on the farm after seeing 'Gay Paree'. The decade is famous for flappers, gun toting rum-runners, neighborhood speakeasies flouting Prohibition, and assembly lines mass-producing a mind-numbing variety and quantity of new consumer goods. The 1920s are portrayed as a rat-a-tat-tat decade of prosperity featuring Coolidge's 'chicken in every pot and a car in every garage.'

The boisterous progress and freedom of the 1920s shine even bolder and brighter against the following decades of the 1930s and 1940s. Grinding poverty during *The* Great Depression and deprivations and death of World War II and its aftermath provide a sobering, gloomy tunnel submerged between the bright ends of the 1920s and the 1950s.

Lost in this brief spin through the past is the story of rapid change and economic wrenching of the U.S. economy during and after World War One. From 1916 through 1920, consumers, producers, savers, and borrowers all tried to adjust to a doubling of prices, which slashed the dollar's real purchasing power in half. After that inflation bubble burst, US residents were whip-sawed with twenty-six months of deflation, falling prices! By March 1923 the price level dropped 23% from its high in December 1920.[3]

From 1916 to 1920, the retail price of one pound of pork chops rose from 22.7 cents to 42.3 cents, falling back to 33 cents in 1922. In the same time periods, a pound of butter went from 39.4 to 70.1 down to 47.9 (all in cents). A pound of potatoes, 27¢ to 63¢ to 28¢. Sugar (lb.), 40¢ to 97¢ to 36¢.[4] Farm incomes tracked this wild ride.

---

[3] U.S. Inflation Calculator and associated data at, http://www.usinflationcalculator.com/inflation/historical-inflation-rates/. Prices for individual goods and commodities could—and often did change more dramatically. For example, wheat prices per bushel, rose 125% from 1915-1919 and then fell 58% from 1919 to 1923. From 1915 to mid-1920 cotton prices rose about 300%, from mid-1920 to June 1921 cotton prices fell 75%.

[4] U.S Department of Commerce, *Historical Statistics of the United States, Colonial Times to 1970*, E187-202, page 213.

Factory (non-farm) incomes did not fluctuate quite as much as farm incomes, but they too took a dizzying ride, rising 98 percent from 1916 to 1920 and falling 27% from 1920 to 1922.[5]

Speaking for cotton growers in particular and farmers in general, John S. Wannamaker, a South Carolina cotton farmer and industry spokesman, testified before Congressional committees on the farm problem. In August of 1921, he blamed the nation's 'bank for banks', the Federal Reserve, for raising its lending rate to commercial banks, making their loans to farmer-customers more expensive and harder to get, consciously following deflationary, price destroying, policies:

> "Federal Reserve Board policies in connection with price and currency deflation are 'cynical, cruel and inexcusable' and constitute 'financial tyranny and commercial criminality',...the Federal board and banks [a]re responsible for the general price decline...' Its policy will require the American people to pay with deflated dollars a national debt borrowed in inflated dollars.'...Mr. Wannamaker asserted that the Federal board and banks were responsible for the general price decline." [6]

At the same time, unemployment rose rapidly from a post-war low of 1.4% to a rate between 15% to 20% in mid-1921; total output fell precipitously by about 20% between early 1920 and mid-1921, and industrial output fell by a whopping 30%.[7] These aggregate averages mask even larger declines in output and greater rises in unemployment in different regions of the country.

This dire post-war period might be better remembered had the 1930s not seen such a lengthy and persistent depression. Yet, brief as it was, the sharp post-World War One depression featured the second largest drop in output in U.S. history and inaugurated "...a complex and stressful decade for most Americans...too often...portrayed as a frivolous era of flappers and flasks à la F. Scott Fitzgerald."[8]

Failing farms and financial ruin helped push over 2.3 million people, one in every twenty, from rural areas to the cities between 1921 and 1923. This accelerated the nation's population tilt from the farm to the cities going from 46% urban — 54% rural in 1900 to 53.3% urban vs. 46.7% rural by 1924.[9] As one commentator concluded: "Clearly, the farm crisis ran deeper than wanderlust at having seen Paris,"[10] helping

---

[5] U.S Department of Commerce, Brissenden, Paul, Earnings of Factory Workers, 1899 to 1927, Table 35, page 93.

[6] *New York Times*, August 23, 1921, page 31. Wannamaker was a South Carolina cotton farmer and founding president of the American Cotton Association, a national organization representing cotton producers.

[7] Miller, N., 2003, pg.87; Vedder and Gallaway, 1993, pps. 61-63.

[8] Romer, 1999, Table 5; the quote from Best, 2003, page x.

[9] http://www.census.gov/population/censusdata/urpop0090.txt

[10] Hansen, J.M., 1991, page 34.

transform the U.S. from Jefferson's agrarian 'nation of small farmers' to a more urban, factory-based, society.

In post-World War One America, returning soldiers did not march straight into the Roaring Twenties, nor was there a chicken in every pot. For most there was no chicken, for many there was no pot, and if they had a garage it was their living space.

This wartime and post-war whipsawing, especially in the value of the currency, was felt everywhere in the country. People experiencing the uncertainty of their purchasing power felt it as soon as they bought the day's meal or other essentials; people borrowing and lending felt it. Capriciously changing price-levels alter the value of what borrowers owe in real terms, inflation reducing their debt and deflation increasing it. Savers' expectations are also frustrated. Inflation lowers their expected receipts and deflation raises them, but only if borrowers can repay. Retirees on fixed-incomes feel the inflation keenly yet have no chance to bargain for wage increases to keep up with the rising prices.

At first, between 1915 and 1920, rapid price inflation reduced the value of savers' and lenders' accounts. They experienced real losses. Then, in 1920-1922, when the price bubble suddenly popped, the unforeseen deflation increased the real value of borrower's debt. This made it more difficult for them to repay. Defaults rose. Creditor-lenders, the Main Street banks in small towns across the country, were now feeling the pain.

Farmers had no problem identifying the culprits pushing farmers off the land.

> "During the war farmers were urged to expand...This requires additional money which our Banker loans us, after getting stocked up money matters tighten up, and Bankers compel us to liquidate our loans...compelled to sell our products...this rush of products floods the market and the bottom drops out of prices...hogs fell from 20 cents Per lb. to 6 cents, cattle 18 cents to 5 cents, corn $2 a bushel in country elevators to 20 cents, wheat $3 bu. to 85 cents, butter fat from 75 cents to 18 cents...this causes the bottom to fall out of farm values...land values are off from 25% to 50% here...the list [of foreclosures] advertised in this Co. filled a full page in our Co, paper...We do not blame our home Banks they are being crowded by K[ansas]C[ity] Bankers who in turn are controlled by Wall St."

> "We have been running on a credit system until the crash. Bankers recalled their loans, business houses refused credit and at the same time asked that our bills be paid up. Result: Jam of all markets, prices going down, farmers unable to buy, stagnation of business all around. No doubt you have been hit also."

> "Confidence and the debt-paying and purchasing power have...been destroyed. Bankruptcies, suicides and the enormous increase in insanity are proof positive of the seriousness of the situation...The suffering of the people is simply appalling. Taxes are unpaid. Thousands and thousands of boys and girls have been called home from

school. Thousands of people who have followed agricultural pursuits all of their lives are giving up in despair and seeking employment elsewhere."[11]

These debtor defaults fueled the rate of bank failures from sixty in 1920 to over 500 in 1921 and the average was almost 700 per year through the rest of the decade.[12]

Throughout its history the U.S. often experienced unpredictable increases and decreases in output. Output slumps were usually caused by droughts, floods, or other natural disasters, leading to crop failures rippling across the broader economy. The drop in output and rising unemployment was reversed when the weather and environment improved and farmers could get back to the crop-cycle. Policy could not prevent natural disasters so governments were typically not looked to for unemployment solutions.

Post-war 'busts' were different. Rather than crop failure causing drops in output, changes to the structure of the economy caused by war production resulted in dislocation and unemployment.

With World War One ending the Federal government quickly terminated contracts for war materials and demobilized over two million servicemen between November 1918 and July 1919. By the end of 1919, numbers in the military had fallen from four million to 130,000.[13] This represented an addition of almost 10% to the labor force.[14]

Federal government spending, which averaged 2.6% of gross domestic product in the twenty-five years preceding World War One, jumped to almost 25% during the War. Immediately upon cessation, $4 billion of contracts, representing 5% of GDP, were cancelled with $2 billion more to follow. By 1921 federal spending had fallen over 70% from $19 billion in 1919 to $5.5 billion. Fiscal tightening![15] This left hundreds of projects across the country, like munitions factories, partially finished, high and dry.

The drop in government spending and re-injection of military personnel into the civilian labor force led to a rapid rise in unemploy-

[11] The first quote from A.W. Rings, Mayetta, KS, to Thomas Edison, April 26, 1922. The second quote, W.L. Vrooman, Ipswich, SD, to Edison, April 6, 1922. The third quote from J.S. Wanamaker to Edison, April 29, 1922. All in TENHP, Banking 1922.

[12] Farm defaults, see: Alston(1983); Alston, Grove and Wheelock (1994) page 411.

[13] Kyvig, 2004, page 6, also: http://www.history.army.mil/books/lineage/M-F/chapter4.htm.

[14] Assuming that all of these demobilized people entered the labor force which numbered 41.5 million in 1920, see http://eh.net/encyclopedia/article/Rockoff.WWI

[15] The word fiscal is derived from the Latin, *fisc*, meaning purse. Thus, *fiscal policy* is the policy of managing the purse—managing the flows of money in and money out. For governments, most often money flows in from taxes and flows out due to expenditure programs.

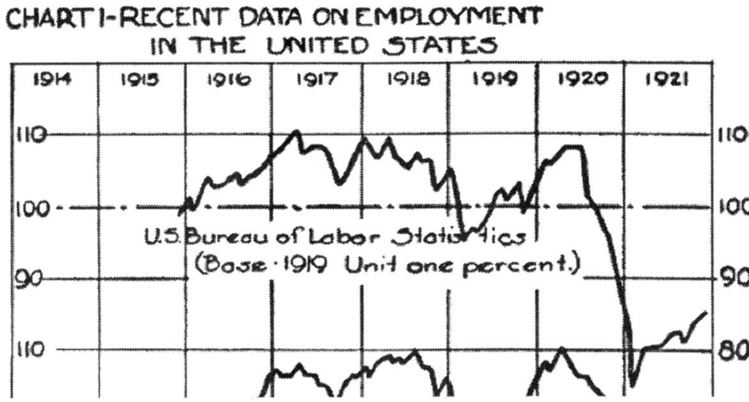

Berridge (1922), page 45.

ment, with upwards of 5.5 million unemployed, about twelve percent of the labor force in 1921.[16] The chart above shows what the people were feeling. Employment, dropping some twenty-five percent from mid-1920 to early 1921, truly was falling 'off the cliff'.

This post-war transition created frictions recognized by the Federal government.

Despite the call for a 'return to normalcy', for the first time, the Federal government was *not* ignoring the unemployment problem. The activist Herbert Hoover, President Harding's Secretary of Commerce, prodded the President to call together scores of prominent academics, representatives from trade, industry, social agencies, and government to investigate the unemployment problem.

Hoover, trained as an engineer, with a successful career of development and invention in the mining industry behind him, spent much of World War One with a private group tirelessly organizing public and private aid efforts for civilians in war-torn Europe. After U.S. entry into the war in 1917, he was responsible for wartime food policy in the U.S. For his immense efforts to feed Europe, he was one of the most decorated and recognized Americans in Europe after the war.

Hoover's efforts at home and abroad were widely hailed. He was approached to run for president by both parties. Running as a Republican, he came up short in the convention. But, he drew notice as a 'doer' and a man of ideas. Harding, quick to invite him in to the cabinet, was surprised when he chose Commerce over the Interior. Hoover planned on turning the young and ill-defined department in to a major presence in government by providing business and industry with in-

[16] Vedder and Gallaway, 1993, page 61. They note that in some months of 1921 unemployment would have been as high as 15%.

formation about local and foreign markets. With Harding's support he expanded the department dramatically, giving it a major role in regulating commerce and the new radio spectrum.

Hoover's experiences in World War One showed him that governments, aid organizations and businesses could be allies, joining to assist those in need. An enemy of waste and inefficiency, he used information to help business and industry rationalize, standardize, and streamline activity. Hoover hoped to minimize swings in economic activity by using the government as an agency reducing uncertainties and frictions through information production, sharing, and coordination activities.

Observing the high and rising level of unemployment through 1921, Hoover asked Harding on August 20, 1921, to convene a "Presidential Commission" to assess and deal with the unemployment situation. This was unprecedented. In previous downturns, the Federal government left employment and the unemployed to the local and state levels. As Edward Eyre Hunt, the secretary of the conference stressed:

> This is the first time there has been a national conference on unemployment called by Federal authorities. In the crisis of 1907, with a president as aggressive and sympathetic as [Theodore] Roosevelt in the White House, the crisis was met, in so far as it was met at all, by private intervention with prominent financiers.
>
> In the crisis of 1914, again with a forward-looking President [Wilson] in the White House, no steps were taken by the Federal Government. The problem of "normal" unemployment — that is, the unemployment characteristic of industry in periods other than cyclical depressions — has never even been discussed at length.[17]

The commission had about sixty high-profile members, chosen from government, business, industry, social agencies, academe, and labor unions. Members included the well-known Hoover, labor leaders John L. Lewis and Samuel Gompers, influential 'muck-raking' journalist Ida Tarbell, Harvard's rising star economist Allyn Young, and the New York Federal Reserve Bank's Benjamin Strong, the most influential banker in the country.

The Conference met from September 26 to October 13, 1921. The conferees worked on reports covering all aspects of unemployment, ranging from a committee on statistics — we need more information — an economic advisory committee, to committees on specific industries, e.g., railroads, shipping, agriculture; and more general issues such as public works and civic emergency measures.

The main charge from Harding and Hoover was that the conference find ways to get Americans employed without drawing on the

[17] Report of the President's Conference on Unemployment, Washington, GPO, 1921, page 171.

federal treasury. Their fear was that the people's self-sufficient ways would be subverted by what they considered charity or a handout.

Harding opened the Conference by stating the prevailing view that, following the distortions of war, peacetime re-adjustments were costly. However, on the whole, they were normal:

> There is always unemployment. Under most fortunate conditions...there are a million and a half in the U.S. who are not at work. The figures are astounding only because we are a hundred millions, and this parasitic percentage is always with us. But there is excessive unemployment to-day...There will be depression after inflation, just as surely as the tides ebb and flow, but we can mitigate, we can shorten duration...We are merely depressed after the fever, and we want to know the way to speediest and dependable convalescence...I would have little enthusiasm for any proposed relief which seeks either palliation or tonic from the public treasury. The excess of stimulation from that source is to be reckoned a cause of trouble rather than a source of cure.[18]

In his opening remarks Hoover stressed that:

> The remedies for these matters must...lie outside of the range of legislation. It is not consonant with the spirit or institutions of the American people that a demand should be made upon the public treasury for the solution of every difficulty...a solution lies in...mobilization of the fine cooperative action of our manufacturers and employers, of our public bodies and local authorities...independence and ability of action amongst our own people...saves our Government from that ultimate paternalism that will undermine our whole political system. In the other countries...solution has been had by direct doles to individuals by their Governments. We have so far escaped this most vicious of solutions... What our people wish is the opportunity to earn their daily bread... we possess the intelligence to find solution. Without it our whole system is open to serious charges of failure.

Conferees produced reports dealing with the immediate, or emergency, unemployment problem and for setting the foundation for the permanent recovery of employment. Reports addressing the emergency situation suggested private and public works construction projects funded through bond sales and the speed-up of already funded, shovel-ready projects. Coordination through local/municipal emergency relief committees and governments assured application of local knowledge. Management groups suggested that costs of production were too high given the falling level of output prices. Labor members argued vociferously against any cut in wages. They threatened to walk out.

---

[18] Ibid, pages 25-27. In 1920, coming off the World War One highs, Federal government expenditures worked out to approximately $700 per person. That was more than three times higher than spending-per-person leading up to World War One, $218 per person in 1900 and $214 in 1910. By 1930, the figure had dropped from the early 1920s level of $700/person to $420/person. In comparison, in 2011, the federal government will spend about $12,500 per person, an increase of about 56 times over the pre-World War One levels. All figures are in 2011 dollars.

The Commission recommended that the Federal government: should be a collector and disseminator of statistical information and, importantly, that it should disentangle itself from the industries taken over during the war. To address the employment situation in the longer run, the Conference recommended actions at the federal level that would lead to more economic certainty for individuals and businesses:

2. Speedy completion of the tax bill...reduction of taxes, in order that business now held back...may proceed.
3. Definite settlement of tariff legislation in order that business may determine its future conduct and policies.
6. Steps looking to the minimizing of fluctuations in exchange, because Recovery...can not make substantial progress so long as extravagant daily fluctuations continue in foreign exchange, for no merchant can determine the delivery cost of any international shipment.
8. ...[T]he rapidity of recovery will depend greatly upon the speed of proportionate adjustment of the inequalities in deflation...It will be observed that agriculture has reached an unduly low plane, ...It will also be observed that there is an entire disproportion between the price of the primary commodities and the ultimate retail price...If the buying power of the different elements of the community is to be restored, then these levels must reach nearer a relative plane....the farmer can not resume his full consuming power and thus give increased employment to the other industries until either his prices increase or until more of the other products and services come into fair balance with his commodities, and therefore the reach of his income.[19]

Hoover concluded the Conference stressing:

> [T]his is a problem for voluntary organization...consonant with the American spirit and...institutions. If we can not secure its solution in that direction we shall have made a distinct step backward in the progress of this country. It is therefore vital that you...should insist...that this is a problem that rests upon the voluntary and neighborly action of the American people...

A month later he said:

> "One of the causes of ill will that weighs heavily upon the community is the whole problem of unemployment...<u>Thirty years ago our business community considered the cyclic financial panic as inevitable. We know now we have cured it through the Federal reserve system</u>. The problem [unemployment] requires study. It, like our banking system, requires a solution consonant with American institutions and thought.[20] (emphasis added)

True to their focus on returning the Federal government to its pre-World War One size in the economy, Federal spending fell from a wartime high of 24% of GDP back towards its pre-war levels of 2.5% of GDP, falling to 3.7% of GDP by mid-decade. Meanwhile, consistent

[19] Ibid, pages 22 and 23. The recommendations 1,4, 5 and 7 dealt with railroad, world armament, and seasonal industry issues.
[20] Ibid, page 170.

with the call from the Unemployment Conference, state and local expenditures rose from 5% of GDP at the end of the war to approximately 8% of GDP by mid-decade (1927). Consequently, total government spending as a proportion of GDP stayed relatively steady at approximately 11.5% of GDP from 1922 through the rest of the 1920s.[21]

Along with the unemployment problem, perhaps causing it, the capricious wartime price inflation-deflation whipsaw was an unwelcome and unexpected intruder. Its painful and surprising appearance certainly was inconsistent with Hoover's claim that it had been 'cured' by the Federal Reserve.

The Civil War inflation and post-war deflation occurred fifty years earlier. By 1921 who remembered? Only one in sixty still lived to recall it. The recent, but brief, Spanish-American War of 1898 caused no observable move in the general level of prices. For the vast majority experiencing the inflation-deflation whipsaw during and after World War One this was their first unpleasant inflation-deflation ride.

In other famous historical episodes, price inflation bubbles fuel legends.[22] Spectacularly affecting the value of a small number of prices, for example tulips in 1630s Holland, or the share prices of a company's stock, as in the 1720s 'South Seas' bubble. These dramatic episodes rarely encompassed the broader price level which is the wartime inflationary experience.

By the early 1920s, in the midst of the inflation-deflation whipsaw, a currency of stable purchasing power — a return to pre-war normalcy was a necessity to stimulate growth and employment. This stable currency would provide a fixed point of value in the U.S. economy for making current and future financial transactions. Without it, as noted in the Conference recommendations, trade would continue to fall and unemployment would continue to rise. The country needed a stable currency.

In Congress, resolutions, bills, and committee hearings were held to look into the 'stable money' problem starting in 1919. Congressmen like T. Alan Goldsborough of Maryland, sponsored 'stable money' bills, with supporters testifying in the hearings. Irving Fisher of Yale University's Economics department was an early advocate of an explicit stable price level provision, appearing frequently before Congressional committees. Princeton's Edwin Kemmerer, the 'international money doctor', was another well-respected and well-known face in Congress.

---

[21] In 2010, the same measure of total government as a proportion of GDP had risen to 44.5%.

[22] Kindleberger, 1989.

Fisher's interest and researches into 'stable money' went back well before the war, appearing in Congress supporting a provision in the Federal Reserve Act of 1913 directing the Federal Reserve Banks to promote a stable price level.[23] Despite Fisher's efforts, this provision did not survive in the bill's ultimate version. Fisher also developed and computed statistical price measures that could be used to judge performance.[24] Thanks to his reputation, his proposals received much public attention.[25]

Post-war, preventing price bubbles and their catastrophic punctures, removing the inflation-deflation whipsaw, was a serious problem needing immediate attention by scholars and Congress. The country needed 'stable' money, money of consistent purchasing power. No matter the source, any proposal promising stable money would have a significant impact on the financial position of the general public, governments at all levels, and all businesses.

At a macro level, as the value of a country's currency becomes less stable and more unpredictable, people lose faith in it and fewer, if any, will accept it. Domestic and foreign trade plummets. As trade falls unemployment rises. Political unrest tends to follow. Governments that preside in times of high and rising inflation and unemployment tend not to win re-election.[26]

Inflation and deflation are bad for businesses as well as individuals. At any time, businesses have accounts receivable and accounts payable. If the purchasing power of the currency is variable, the business's liabilities (payables) and assets (receivables) may be whipsawed around quite rapidly and capriciously. Depending on scheduled dates of receipt and payment, there is no guarantee that the value of receivables and payables will rise and fall together. This uncertainty about future

---

[23] Fisher authored a major work on the question, *The Purchasing Power of Money*, in 1911.

[24] Fisher, 1934, pps. 148-151.

[25] Fisher was also a bit of a 'self-promoter' with detractors among the public. 'L.E. Billson' of Cleveland, OH, wrote to J.S. Wannamaker: "I have no confidence in Irving Fisher... Mr. Fisher is a book agent and not a political economist. I have written him a half dozen letters calling his attention to the ancient political economy which he is imposing upon the students of Yale in exchange for the salary which he receives from the millionaire supporters of Yale College. It seems strange that Professor Fisher talks of stabilizing the value of money with one breath and then refuses to stabilize it in its most important aspect, that is, the interest rate for money. He betrays his whole case in proposing to allow the interest rate to be a matter of free trade among the bankers and to be such rate as they think will most successfully rob their victims." May 31, 1922. Copy sent to Edison by J.S. Wannamaker, in Banking 1922, TENHP.

[26] A list of countries suffering political instability to the point of government collapse due to inflationary episodes is long, some notable cases: Germany, Austria and other middle European countries in the early 1920s, Hungary (1946), mainland China and Taiwan, 1948-1949, Argentina in the 1980s, Brazil in the late 1980s-early 1990s, Zimbabwe, 2002-2008.

price changes keeps businesses from making long-term commitments that may turn against them causing losses.

What was the nation's bank, The Federal Reserve System, that Hoover famously said had "cured" cyclical swings, doing? The Governor of the System, W.P.G. Harding — the Ben Bernanke of his day — pointed to it as a source of strength and stability.[27] In a lengthy speech he noted that there had been no "money panic" since the System's inception.[28] He identified the sources of deflation as 'potent public opinion' against rising prices leading to a "buyer's strike", and that despite the Fed's actions to boost credit there was

> "no clear and immediate relationship between commodity prices and the volume of credit and currency…it involves other factors…the volume of trade and production, the rapidity of turnover or velocity of exchange and likewise public confidence." He also cautioned that the Fed's role was not to "attempt to fix or control prices."

Implying that conditions would have been even worse, Harding asked attendees to imagine what would have happened in the economy in the absence of Fed action.[29]

He then explained that the Fed believed that money creation was driven by the level and changes in business activity. That the demand for credit and currency worked through the local banks to the Fed, which acted passively, to expand currency in times of rising business activity, and decreasing it when the demand of trade were depressed.[30] He ended his speech with a verse from poet Edward Everett Hale:

> "Look up and not down,
> Look forward and not back,
> Look out and not in,

[27] The Governor of the Federal Reserve Board in Washington, D.C., was the leading public official in the Federal Reserve System. Despite a similar name, W.P.G. Harding — an Alabama banker — was not related to President W.G. Harding.

[28] The Federal Reserve System, which encompasses the Board in Washington, D.C., and the twelve Federal Reserve District banks and their owners, thousands of 'local' banks across the country, is often referred to as "the Fed." Harding's speech, "Credit, Currency and Business," was addressed to the Southern Wholesale Dry Goods Association, Birmingham, AL, May 10, 1922. Copy in Banking 1922, TENHP.

[29] This, of course, sounds quite modern and is a 'defense' of almost any policy as long as one can imagine horrendous enough counter-factual possibilities.

[30] This is a passive, 'real bills', approach to monetary policy. With "real bills" being the loans that local banks have made to businesses. Local banks (if they were members of the Fed System) could then present these loans to the Fed and use them as collateral for a loan from the Fed.

Lend a hand."[31]

With prices falling by about 10 percent per year, unemployment well over 10%, was the "unemployment" commission recommending *local* action and the Fed recommending a poetic *"Lend a hand"* the best that the Federal government could do? Many, including Thomas Edison — 'The Greatest Man in America' — thought not.[32]

In late 1921 Thomas Edison addressed the currency problem with more than a big businessman's myopic concern. Unlike other proposals for the currency, Edison's was stimulated by his close friend's, Henry Ford's, proposal to buy federal government assets. With names like *Edison* and *Ford*, it is no surprise that public attention was immediate and intensely focused on Edison's project.

Edison and Ford first met at a dinner given for Edison in Detroit in 1896. Edison was by then a household name for his inventive genius, Ford an unknown working as a mechanic-engineer for the Edison Illuminating Company in Detroit. At that dinner Edison enthusiastically encouraged Ford's work on the internal combustion engine. Ford never forgot this encouragement. Thirteen years later, when Ford visited his laboratory unannounced, Edison encouraged him yet again, this time to stick through a lawsuit against a Detroit group holding monopoly rights to engine patents. Ford would ultimately prevail in the case and credited Edison's guidance.

After that, Ford and Edison grew close, with the younger Ford almost idolizing Edison and Edison respecting Ford. Ford tried to work Edison's batteries in to the Model T and even in to an electric car. The Ford's vacationed with the Edison's in Fort Myers, Florida, first in 1914 and later they bought property near by. In October 1915, after visiting the Panama-Pacific Exposition in San Francisco, Ford took Edison to Santa Rosa to meet Luther Burbank. Ford, Edison, the poet John Burroughs, and the tire-maker, Harvey Firestone went on well publicized 'camping trips' in 1916, 1918, and 1919. Of Ford, Edison wrote in 1916:

> "...while mankind appears to have been gradually drifting into an artificial life of merciless commercialism, there are still a few who have not been caught in the meshes of this frenzy and who are still human and enjoy the wonderful panorama of the mountains, the valleys and the plain, with their wonderful content of living things,

[31] Edison read the speech in 1922. He found it wanting. He has many comments written in the margins of his copy. In the section where Harding claimed there had been "no money panic" he wrote: "Okay, what is it we have now?"
[32] *New York Times*, July 23, 1922, page 84.

and among these persons I am proud to know my two friends, John Burroughs and Henry Ford." [33]

At first, Edison's work on money in 1921 seemed motivated by his friend's highly publicized and controversial proposal to purchase government wartime assets. Public interest and scrutiny was immediate. However, for Edison, his research was more than window-dressing for his friend's proposal. His researches and efforts were aimed at assistance in times of need:

> "We ought to do something about the farmer. It's a moral obligation. He doesn't know anything about figures. He gets skinned."[34]

Edison's proposal, first made publicly in off the cuff remarks in a remote location, then refined through a period of time as he 'burned the midnight oil', put the full force of his creative thought and inventiveness on display. After reading his proposal and speaking with him, the scholarly and erudite Fisher complimented him, inviting him to present his ideas to Congress.

Naturally, Edison's proposal generated enormous public interest at the time because of who he was and what he meant to the average person. He lit your world after sundown. He brought moving pictures to the theater near you. He developed the 'talking machine' through which you listened — whenever *you chose* — to popular entertainers 'in' your home. If that short list of achievements is all you knew of him, it was long enough so that almost everyone on the globe felt his presence. With his record of achievement, you probably shared his full faith and conviction that he could also bring you and the nation money of stable purchasing power. He vowed to stabilize money's purchasing power: "I want to cast the variable out of money!"[35]

As Edison knew, money and purchasing power are important to everyone, not just farmers or bankers or industrialists. This makes Edison's quest to re-engineer the U.S. monetary system more than an interesting tale of a famous inventor knocking about in unfamiliar territory. Many threads have to be disentangled and then woven together in this story.

The first thread is an analysis of the monetary system of the day. It was just a few short years earlier that the federal government and Congress, building on voluminous contributions from the academic community, carefully planned changes to the monetary system that were embodied in the Federal Reserve Act of 1913. What was the sys-

---

[33] Quoted in Josephson (a959), page 460. For much more on the Edison-Ford friendship see Josephson (1959), chapter XXII.

[34] *New York Times*, Section Seven, page 1, July 16, 1922.

[35] *New York Times*, Section Seven, page 1, July 16, 1922.

tem and why did it fail just a few short years later to protect against purchasing power instability?

A second thread winds around the different interests of different members of the economy. Savers, or their representatives, e.g. bankers, should feel differently about a system that may be inherently inflationary than they feel about a system that may be inherently deflationary. Borrowers may have the opposite view of the benefits and costs of inflation versus deflation. Were the old, new, and Edison's proposed system inherently unstable in one, or both, directions?

The third thread is familiar to anyone conversant with the monetary history of the U.S.: a visceral fear of control of money being given over to either 'big city', typically Philadelphia or New York City, bankers, or that control being concentrated with the federal government in Washington, D.C. Who was in control and who did Edison want in control?

A complete tapestry featuring the tensions and disputes that make the parts of it glow and shimmer gives us the knowledge to understand the strengths and weaknesses of monetary systems, then and now. The story of the early 1920s and the great inventor's search for stable money illuminates Edison's correspondence with those interested in the 'money complex'. He corresponded with wheat and corn farmers in the Midwest, cotton growers in the south, bankers and financiers in major cities, well-known academics in the best universities in the country, government officials, and Civil War veterans.

It seemed as if everyone had a story and an opinion for him. Some of them influenced Edison, and Edison sought to influence them. Through it all, Edison kept a careful governor on his feelings, holding to his disciplined engine of invention and innovation that had proven its success time and again.

Work on this new invention, stable money, started accidentally in late 1921, thanks to a journey with his friend Henry Ford. 'The Flivver King' was taking him to the deep south to see an abandoned dam site. How is this going to make money 'good'? How is this going to stabilize the nation's prices? When he accepted Ford's offer the questions had never occurred to Edison. After the trip he could think of little else.

CHAPTER 3: RESCUE MISSION ON THE BANKS OF THE TENNESEE

The journey starts at noon on Friday, December 2, 1921, at the Ford siding of the Michigan Central Railroad in Dearborn, Michigan. Ford and Edison, two of America's most famous and chronicled men step quickly through the blustery westerly winds and sporadic rain into Ford's private rail car, the "Fair Lane". Also, traveling with them are a small group of Ford engineers and Ford's twenty-eight year-old son, Edsel.

Part of the trip rolls over rails Ford has recently purchased. When they look out at dusty paths and highways the car they see moving Americans is Ford's Model T. Passing houses in the evening hours, the electric light shining out to them is thanks to Edison. Traveling south and slightly towards the west, they travel about 700 miles, arriving in the morning hours of Saturday, December 3, 1921.

While enjoying spending time together and despite the rural destination, this trip is not one their famous "camping" trips. This is all business and all Ford's business. They will stay as long as necessary. Ford spends part of the journey south 'schooling' Edison in his plans; at the end of this line there will be townsmen and press to meet and statements to be made. Ford wants and Ford needs 'America's Most Useful Citizen' well prepared.[36]

Listening carefully, Edison has every confidence in his Ford's ideas and is eager to see the site. He has faith that his younger friend will transform the sleepy lands bordering these bends in the Tennessee River into a productive engine just as he had transformed Highland Park and was in the process of transforming the land along the River Rouge in and around Detroit. True to Ford's plan and Edison's hopes, this day will change the lives of millions of Americans, but not at all in the way that Ford plans.

For his part, Thomas Edison will never forget the banks and bends of the Tennessee River, for it is here that he is unknowingly about to launch into an invention unlike any he has carried out before.

Stepping out of the "Fair Lane" the group enjoys unseasonably warm weather while making their way to the Wilson Dam across the Tennessee River. The dam, started in 1918 as part of the nation's wartime munitions program, is unfinished. Work on it halted in mid-construction when the war ended. At the height of construction over 18,000 workers and their families lived in the nearby towns of Florence,

[36] Josephson, 1959, page 460.

Sheffield, Tuscumbia, and Muscle Shoals. The larger area known as 'The Shoals' and according to the press of the day the object of Ford's desire is sited at Muscle Shoals.[37]

The end of the war in November 1918 came two weeks before production of the first ammonium nitrate explosives at Muscle Shoals. With cessation of hostilities, there was no need for explosives. Without a need for ammonium nitrates there was no need for a dam to generate electricity to produce the explosives or power the towns the workers would have occupied.

The federal government's strategy to return to its smaller, normal, pre-war presence in the economy included selling unneeded assets. In July, four months earlier, Ford offered to buy the Wilson Dam for $5 million if the government would complete its construction. Ford and his engineers envisioned a city stretching for 75 miles along the banks of the Tennessee occupied by residents producing fertilizer in the now abandoned ammonium nitrate plants all powered by the Wilson Dam.[38]

Ford believed that he was providing the federal government with a guarantee of success along the Tennessee. The name 'Ford' was synonymous with industry, efficiency, reliability, and trust. He was staking his name on a project that promised employment for thousands, cheap fertilizer for the nation's farmers, lower food prices for the citizenry, and higher economic growth. All of this at a time when the country appeared to be mired in a post-war slump, with no obvious way out, and with the government holding useless war-driven 'assets' that were rusting and decaying in place. One more year along the humid Tennessee and the scrap value of the Wilson Dam and its munitions plants would fall even farther.

The project "became a national craze…another California gold rush...Ford made it a symbol of hope for farmers everywhere."... *"I want Ford to Get Muscle Shoals"* buttons were sold…"[39]

Yet, completing the dam would cost the federal government an estimated, additional $68 million.[40] Ford proposed that the government use a novel financing plan and President Harding seemed very willing to consider it favorably.[41] Congress, for the most part, also seemed willing. To generate public support, Ford and the engineers will explain the dream, show Edison the dam and mothballed plants, wait for his —

[37] "The History of the City of Muscle Shoals", http://www.cityofmuscleshoals.com/Default.asp?ID=11; also, the *New York Times*, December 6, 1921, page 6.
[38] Lacey, 1986, *Ford*, page 212.
[39] Lacey, 1986, pps. 211-212.
[40] That's about $900 million in 2011 dollars.
[41] Lacey, op. cit.

hoped for — favorable comments and then ride the tide of public support to a successful agreement with the government.

After an 8 A.M. inspection of the mothballed munitions plants in Sheffield on Monday, December 5, Ford and Edison meet with townspeople in Florence, shake hands and muss the hair of excited schoolchildren and give autographs on their way. In Florence, Ford gave a brief speech to the Chamber of Commerce and the press. Then Edison spoke and answered questions before the team returned north in the "Fair Lane".

This event was of national prominence and Ford must have been greatly pleased with the press coverage. Carried in the pages of *New York Times*, the press conference and coverage must have buoyed Ford's hopes.[42] Reporting to the nation, the esteemed Edison fully describes every advantage of the plan. Edison appears neutral, guileless and without having any personal benefit in the scheme.

Two elements of Ford's proposal drew the most public attention: the offer price of $5 million and his financing scheme. Some in Congress felt that $5 million was ridiculously low given the $85 million the project had cost to-date. An estimate of the scrap value of the abandoned facilities was $8 million, $3 million greater than Ford's offer price.[43] Furthermore, people were skeptical about Ford's suggestion that the government should pay another $68 million for the dam's completion by issuing a new type of money.

The typical way a government would raise the funds necessary for a large project is either by taxation or by borrowing. Borrowing — or *debt financing* — is done by selling bonds in the capital markets. Bonds are promises to repay the lenders their principal and a stream of interest. Ford suggested that the federal government should eliminate debt financing and print Federal Reserve notes — paper money currency — to pay for the necessary expenses. These notes would be retired by the Federal Reserve as the power from the dam came on stream, was delivered to all those families, and as they paid for it.

In his view, no lender and no interest payments means cheaper financing for the government and the taxpayers. But, some asked: What 'backed' this currency? Where was the gold that backed other dollars? Is this for Ford's advantage and the government's disadvantage? Is there weight and legitimacy to such a currency?

Paper dollars were viewed skeptically given how quickly they could become worthless. People only accepted them because they could exchange, or convert, them in to gold. During the Revolutionary War, the Continental Congress issued inconvertible paper currency and it

---

[42] *New York Times*, December 6, 1921, page 6.

[43] Lacey, 1986, op. cit.

was still infamous in the phrase "Not worth a Continental" meaning an item was worthless. During the Civil War, too, paper currency known for its color as "greenbacks" was issued. It was not convertible in to gold. These dollars quickly lost value, too, and were worked in to song and folklore.[44]

In 1921, the rate of exchange of paper currency to gold was $20.67 for an ounce of gold. Where was the gold that would stand behind this new paper currency Ford suggested that the government print?

The *Times* reported Edison giving his listeners three reasons for accepting Ford's proposal. First, under Ford's dynamic leadership, the location and existing plants would provide the ability to make munitions (if they were not making peacetime fertilizer) in quantities and at such speed deterring any country from attacking the U.S.

> "...without hesitation. It would be the greatest insurance against war that we have. Second[ly]...Ford is known as a great manufacturer...He is the one logical man to do this thing. Third[ly] — The whole country has an abiding faith that Ford will not operate it to get every dollar possible out of it for himself. He will make it an American institution, doing the greatest good for the greatest possible number."

Edison firmly endorsed Ford's 'create-currency-pay-no-interest' financing plan. After expressing faith in local banks and banking, Edison stressed

> "It is the money broker, the money profiteer, the private banker, that I oppose. They gain their power through a fictitious and false value given to gold. Gold is a relic of Julius Caesar and interest is an invention of Satan."

For financing public projects Edison observed,

> "Then there is another way — the method [of] my friend Ford...He proposes to just go along and forget about gold. He says that the Government can finance Muscle Shoals without applying to money brokers for permission and I think he is absolutely right about it."

"But," he was asked, "would not Mr. Ford's suggestion that Muscle Shoals be financed by a currency issue raise some objection?" Edison retorted,

> "Certainly. There is a complete set of misleading slogans kept on hand for just such outbreaks of common sense among the people...There would be new shrieks of 'fiat money' and 'paper money' and 'greenbackism,' and all the rest of it — the same old cries with which the people have been shouted down from the beginning...Maybe

---

[44] Smithsonian Folkways, 2007, CD. *If You Ain't Got the Do-Re-Mi: Songs of Rags and Riches.* http://media.smithsonianfolkways.org/liner_notes/smithsonian_folkways/SFW40195.pdf

they can't shout down American thinkers any longer. The only dynamite that works in this country is the dynamite of a sound idea."

"Now here is Ford proposing to finance Muscle Shoals by an issue of currency. Very well, let us suppose for a moment Congress follows his proposal. Personally, I don't think Congress has imagination enough to do it, but let us suppose that it does. The required sum is authorized — say $30,000,000. The bills are issued directly by the Government, as all money ought to be....They will be the same as any other currency put out by the Government: that is, they will be money. They will be based on the public wealth already in Muscle Shoals, and their circulation will increase that public wealth, not only the public money but the public wealth — real wealth."

" When these bills have answered the purpose of building and completing Muscle Shoals, they will be retired by the earnings of the power dam. That is, the people of the United States will have all that they put into Muscle Shoals and all that they can take out for centuries — the endless wealth-making water power of that great Tennessee River—with no tax and no increase of the national debt."

Asked, "But suppose Congress does not see this, what then?"

"Well, Congress must fall back on the old way of doing business. It must authorize an issue of bonds. That is, it must go out to the money brokers and borrow enough of our own national currency to complete great national resources, and we must then pay interest to the money brokers for the use of our own money."

"Now, that is what Henry Ford wants to prevent. He thinks it is stupid, and so do I, that for the loan of $30,000,000 of their own money the people of the United States should be compelled to pay $66,000,000 — that is what it amounts to, with interest. People who will not turn a shovelful of dirt nor contribute a pound of material will collect more money from the United States than will the people who supply the material and do the work. That is the terrible thing about interest."

"It is absurd to say that our country can issue $30,000,000 in bonds and not in currency. Both are promises to pay, but one promise fattens the usurer, and the other helps the people...The people must pay anyway; why should they be compelled to pay twice, as the bond system compels them to pay?"

Asked: "Are you going to have anything to do with outlining this proposed policy?" Edison responded:

"I am just expressing my opinion as a citizen...Ford's idea is flawless. They won't like it. They will fight it, but the people of this country ought to take it up and think about it. I believe it points the way to many reforms and achievements which cannot come under the old system."

With that they swung aboard the "Fair Lane" heading north. They made a stop at Andrew Jackson's home, The Hermitage, near Nashville, Tennessee, on their return journey to Michigan. This was a particularly apt stop. After all, Jackson's own battles with 'big city' bankers and money-men were well-known and contributed to his presidential election. Ford was rumored to have similar ambitions.

Ford was undoubtedly pleased with his Edison's understanding of the proposal and strong, logical-sounding, defense and advocacy. For both men, that visit to Muscle Shoals would be a memorable event. For Ford, the highly public attempt to buy the Wilson Dam launches him even more prominently into the public eye. Yet, his high-profile attempt to drive public opinion also brings a nasty surprise.

Suspicious of Ford's motives and believing that large projects should be handled by government and not "profiteers," Robert Norris, a U.S. Senator from Nebraska and chairman of the Senate Agricultural Committee, launched a counter-attack to Ford's plan. He believed governments should provide public projects not sell their assets to private industrialists. He and a small, but vociferous group, battled to prevent the government from selling the Wilson Dam to Ford.

This battle brought Norris far from Nebraska and Washington, D.C., to rural Alabama and the Tennessee River Valley. Appalled at the poverty, Norris became a major force in the Senate for the 1930s legislation creating the Tennessee Valley Authority (TVA) and the Rural Electrification Act (REA). While Ford ultimately gave up his interest in the Wilson Dam, withdrawing his offer in 1924, the intense scrutiny his offer brought to bear on the region forever altered the rural landscapes and economies in the southeast through the TVA, which included the Wilson Dam, and across the country via the REA.[45] Without Ford's aggressive offer and Norris's counter-offensive, these large-scale projects may never have been built.

For Edison, the 'money' storm broke almost immediately. His widely quoted comments on Ford's financing plan, and his comments on banking in general, were quickly addressed by two well-known writers in the New York financial press, Henry Hazlitt and Henry Parker Willis.[46]

Over low heat, Hazlitt roasted Edison in his column in the *New York Evening Mail* of December 9, writing:

"Edison is not given to asinine statements. His mind is immensely broader than Ford's; he is more balanced, less one-sided; he has a saving strain of common sense and of humor; he has read vastly more and is therefore not so subject to Ford's vagaries. When he essays with the utmost confidence to speak *ex cathedra* upon the subject of

---

[45] See Grandin, Greg, *Fordlandia- The Rise and Fall of Henry Ford's Forgotten Jungle City,* 2009, Picador, New York, Henry Holt and Co., PPS. 65-68,75-80,102-107,257-262.

[46] Hazlitt at that time was the Financial Editor of the *New York Evening Mail,* previously he had written for the *Wall Street Journal.* Hazlitt, in a long career, would write over twenty books, write for just about every New York City paper including the *New York Times*, influential magazines (e.g., *The Nation, Newsweek*), and was a founder of the Foundation for Economic Education. Willis at that time was a professor of banking at Columbia University, editor in chief of the *Journal of Commerce*, and the Director of Research, Federal Reserve Board. He worked for Congressman Carter Glass in 1912 and 1913 on the drafting of the Federal Reserve Act and had made international trips advising foreign governments on their monetary systems.

currency, his remarks are at least not so grotesque and puerile as Ford's gibberish. They even wear a certain air of plausibility. There are flashes of true insight. Nevertheless, taken as a whole they are arrant nonsense.

They prove that even one of the greatest geniuses in the world, when he moves out of his own field and enters into a field in which men for generations have specialized and given their whole lives to thinking on its problems, making false starts and correcting them through experience and critical intelligence — when even the greatest genius in the world ventures into such a subject in an offhand way, contemptuous of all that has been done before him, he is bound to make a sorry picture.

Even Edison's fallacies are not original. His mistakes are the old, old mistakes, the perennial mistakes, the mistakes that have raised their heads every year and been demolished every year, from times long before the old colonial days, when the Continental currency of the American Revolution, after falling in value more and more until it circulated for a time at rates of from $500 to $1,000 for $1 in gold...

It is astounding when one thinks of it. After all the terrible agonies of paper money through which the world has passed, after our own American revolutionary currency, after the John Law currency in France, the assignats of the French revolution, our own Civil war greenbacks, after the horrors of paper money now raging in Germany, in Austria, in Poland, in Russia, it is still possible, not for a few obscure cranks or inmates of asylums but for men of high public standing and immense accomplishment, to advocate paper money...

Of course, Mr. Edison's suggestion is "different". Such suggestions, in the minds of their proposers, always are. Mr. Edison would be astonished if he took such a book, say, as the late Andrew D. White's *Paper Money Inflation in France* and read the arguments eloquently set forth by the Frenchmen of 1796 when they proposed to begin their paper money issues that turned out so disastrously. Does Mr. Edison think that they proposed to issue billions to begin with? No; their first issue was...very modest, and they were going to limit it to that. But, alas, these things do not control themselves...

But, the task of supplying Mr. Edison with an economic education cannot be undertaken in a newspaper article. It is a task for a book or for many books, and there are many competent ones if Mr. Edison cares to read them. He is so prodigiously useful a man in his own sphere that he does not need to study economics. But if he feels called upon to dismiss all the accumulated body of thought that economists have built up and give public interviews advocating a revolution of our currency system he owes it not only to the public safety but to his own reputation to find out at least what the thoughts that he dismisses are and on what grounds they are based."[47]

In a December 14 speech to the New York Credit Men's Association, Willis said the idea is "old like a good many of Ford's ideas," adding that Edison "would approve the issuance of the notes provided Ford or anyone else could guarantee that the power representing the collateral would be produced. But he condemned the proposition be-

[47] December 9, 1921, *The New York Evening Mail*, "Business and Finance by Henry Hazlitt", copy in TENHP, Banking 1921. On his copy Edison has circled the section dealing with Andrew D. White's book and instructs: "Meadowcroft, get this book."

cause by it the Government would be 'giving to certain people the power to consume things needed by the community.'"[48]

The quick negative responses stung Edison. But, they did not stop him. Intrigued by Ford's proposal to remove interest from the payments system and remove the Wall Street 'money-brokers' from control, Edison decided that it was time he study the money question seriously with the same discipline and resources he researched any promising new idea. With over one thousand patents for physical, electromechanical, and other types of goods and processes, he was just the one to show the world the flaws in the gold standard and the Federal Reserve. But he would not stop there. He would prove those critics wrong. He would design a stable currency system providing 'the dynamite of a sound idea' and 'banish Satan' from the nation's finance.

[48] *New York Times*, page 26, Dec. 15, 1921.

CHAPTER 4: GOLD? GREAT CAESAR'S GHOST!

Gold a relic? Interest an invention of Satan? Edison's words rang out in Florence and reverberated through a country that was reeling from the inflation-deflation whipsaw. All debtors, owing principal *and* interest, read Edison's words carefully. Criticism of gold was not new. Some still heard William Jennings Bryan's ringing cry of 1896 echoing: "You shall not press down upon the brow of labor this crown of thorns, you shall not crucify mankind upon a cross of gold."

Why were these men railing against gold? Why did Edison damn interest to Hell? Was it because he had a history of close financial 'calls' needing almost-emergency financing for one invention or another? Getting his inventions perfected and to market often required some complicated financial engineering involving:

"...rival 'barons'...such as the Goulds and the Vanderbilts...In this strange financial warfare, this ceaseless maneuvering and intriguing of the money lords of the Gilded Age, Edison the technician, would be unwittingly and hopelessly involved—nay pulled hither and thither, as he tried to serve first one side and then the other, until he himself would scarcely know where he was, or if he owned his own soul."[49]

Personal feelings of financiers aside, Edison concluded that it was not these men that were the problem. Answering one Kansas farm correspondent he writes:

"The farmer's trouble is not due to Wall Street, nor to speculators, nor to bankers. It is due to a bad system of money...Everything that eastern men do would be done by the farmer himself if he could...we are all gamblers by nature. If a system of checks can be worked out, and I think it can, the farmer will get justice."[50]

Writing of inflation-deflation to a South Carolina cotton grower he offered:

"The farmers everywhere, and not alone the farmers but all people not knowing the laws of money, naturally thought they were highly prosperous and on that basis contracted debts. These debts were contracts on low value money and will have to be paid in money of greater value....All these troubles are due to our banking system and the very poor supervision over the actions of banks."[51]

---

[49] Josephson (1959), page 104. Though he may not have been the financial naïf as sometimes portrayed, e.g. see Conot (1979), page 465. These, and the biographies by Baldwin (1995) and Israel (1998), all contain much more content on Edison's interrelationships and financial dealings with the men and institutions of his time including Jay Gould, J.P. Morgan, the Vanderbilts, etc.

[50] Edison to A.W. Rings, May 9, 1922. TENHP Banking 1922.

[51] Edison to J.S. Wannamaker, May 6, 1922. TENHP Banking 1922.

Just what sort of goofy monetary system did the U.S. have anyway? According to Edison on that warm day in Florence, the monetary system we had in 1921 was ignorantly based on gold. Gold that was being manipulated and controlled by the 'money brokers, money profiteers, and private bankers'.

"The probable reason it [gold] is retained as the basis of money is that it is easy to control. And it is the control of money that constitutes the money question. It is the control of money that is the root of all evil...Money ought to be plentiful. It would be plentiful if it were mined in as large quantities as it could be, but an artificial scarcity is maintained by those who use gold to monopolize money."[52]

So, this is where Edison started, parting with the well-satisfied Ford in Detroit and returning to New Jersey. After all, engineering something better, like a better light bulb, required knowing where and how the current item was faulty. Why should the approach to improving the monetary system be any different? He would put the monetary system on the 'test bench' and investigate, writing: "I am studying the whole question starting with the first recorded panics in Europe and to-date, and hope some day to get something out of the Complex which may be of some value, there appear to be many conflicting opinions."[53]

The system Edison put on the test bench to study was complicated, to get an idea of what it looked like let's build it up in steps starting with a basic version. Up to World War One most countries had monetary systems based on gold. The quantity of gold in a country limited the amount of money that could circulate. Visualize the country's gold stock minted into coins. These coins circulate in exchange for goods and services.

Prices are determined for goods and services by the usual market supply and demand considerations for each of the goods and services. To get a quick idea of what is happening to prices *in general*, we can make up a formula using all of the individual prices. This is a *price index* representing the average level of prices, or *the* price level.[54]

Any individual price may change due to changes in demand or supply. However, if the quantity of gold remains constant, the price index will remain unchanged. If our demand for one good rises, its price rises and we spend more gold coins on it. We then have fewer

---

[52] *New York Times*, Dec. 6, 1921, page 6.

[53] Note to Pierre Jay (New York Federal Reserve Bank), April 1922, in Banking, TENHP Archives.

[54] A price index is an average, a synthetic composite where one number represents many numbers. There are a number of different price indices. The simplest might be the arithmetic average of all prices. The *wind chill* factor is an analogous concept where air temperature and wind speed are combined by a formula in to one composite number. If air temperature falls and wind speed also falls, the wind chill factor may remain unchanged.

gold coins to spend on other goods and services, their prices fall. So, the price level, the index representing the average of prices remains unchanged and total economic activity is unchanged.

We can show this as follows, the amount of gold, represented by the size of the pyramid determines the amount of money in the economy. Prices are set by demand and supply, these prices may be aggregated in to a price index representing the price level which is shown (arbitrarily) equal to 100.

Buried within the changes in relative demands are sectoral shifts in the economy. Some industries are born and grow while others decline. The industry experiencing the demand increase views times as 'booming'. Industries experiencing demand decreases see a bust, panic, or depression. Overall, economic activity is unchanged.

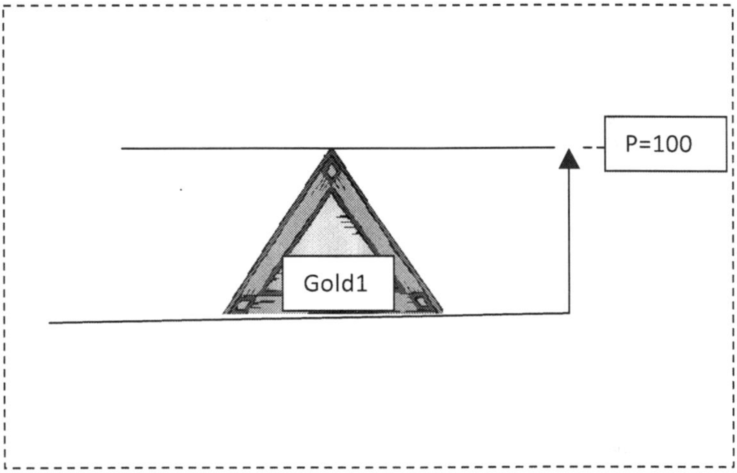

The gold supply, Gold1, supports a price level P = 100.

If the quantity of gold and gold coins changes, for example, rises, then we have more gold coins to spend on at least one good without reducing our spending on other goods or services. In this case, the price index rises. [55]

[55] This has happened in history, perhaps most famously in sixteenth-century Europe, see Fischer, *The Great Wave*, 1996.

In the following chart the gold supply, Gold 1, supports a price level P=100. If the gold supply doubles to Gold 2, the price level doubles to P=200.

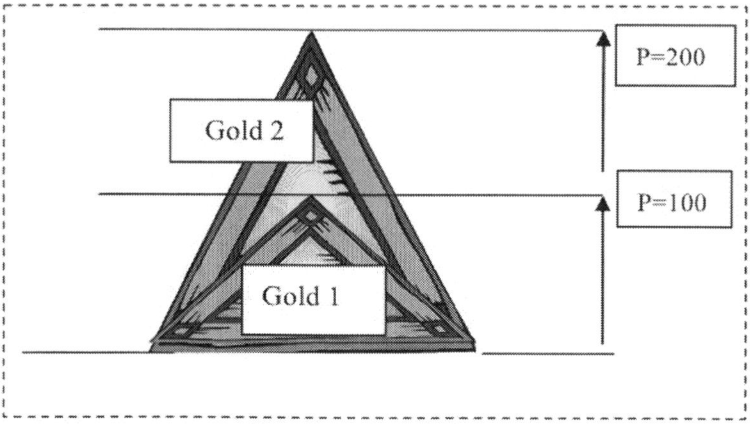

If the quantity of gold falls, then the price index falls. The entire economy seemingly experiences a boom or a bust. Gold acts as an automatically operating anchor controlling the country's price level. The price *level* changes only if the quantity of gold changes.

What happens if we expand this to more than one country? Not much. If both countries have roughly the same goods and services for sale, gold is spent where the goods are cheapest and flows away from the country where goods are more expensive. These flows act to equalize the prices and price levels in terms of gold in both countries.[56] Again, gold flows automatically anchoring price levels in all countries. This is the system's *golden rule.*

However, it does not happen overnight. It takes time for people to realize where the higher and lower prices are, for the gold and goods to pass each other on ships in the night, and the price levels to re-equilibrate across nations. In normal times, these flows happen day-by-day, in small amounts, and the adjustments are being made continuously. In those countries toward which the gold is flowing, economic

[56] The philosopher David Hume is credited with one of the first expositions of the stabilizing effect of what he termed the international price-specie flow mechanism. We are simplifying away transportation costs of gold and goods and assuming that most goods are tradable.

activity is stimulated (as in our xample), and in countries from which gold is flowing, economic activity slows.[57]

What if times are not normal? Could interruptions or interferences create situations where a generalized inflation and then deflation, the inflation-deflation whipsaw follows? Looking at this test-bench model Edison saw that the whipsaw was possible. Let war break out. A country at war mobilizes resources to fight. Governments come in as a significant demander of goods and services. These governments may also borrow internationally in order to help their war effort. All of this borrowing causes gold to flow towards that country and its price level rises. Typically, wartime shipping is interrupted, less secure, and limited to war material. Inflation results and persists. After the war, debt repayment and the normal price-gold flows will cause gold to flow out of that country and its price level should decline. Deflation.

The *golden rules* of the gold standard mean that inflationary booms are followed by deflationary 'busts'. Often the language used is more colorful, the 'painful hangovers' following the 'rip-snorting parties', "There will be depression after inflation, just as surely as the tides ebb and flow," and the like. Why must deflation follow? Why does the gold standard prevent *laissez les bon temps rouler*? The answer is two-fold: theory and evidence. (Turn the page to see some relevant chart data from earlier post-war periods in U.S. history.)

[57] Hume noted this transitional effect on business activity, too.

This boom-bust pattern is evident in the two nineteenth-century wars involving the U.S. Consider, in the following chart, consumer price index data for the period surrounding the War of 1812:[58]

And here is what happened to the price level in the period surrounding the Civil War:

What is evident is that the price level rose in wartime and fell following the cessation of hostilities.[59] The immediate post-war periods

[58] The War of 1812 was declared in June of 1812 by the U.S. and ended with the ratification of the Treaty of Ghent in February 1815.

were also ones of higher unemployment and economic hardship. Edison didn't need any musty old books to recall this whipsaw happening during and after the Civil War. He was there. He was 'Young Al', a teenager, working the trains and writing and selling newspapers at the start of the war — business boomed! — and later, in the post-war bust, a telegrapher and inventor scrambling to keep afloat.[60]

In both post-war periods, the federal government's response to the busts was embodied in various acts opening up territory for expansion. In both periods, land was cheap — if not free — and available. The frontiers were still being pushed westward. If a man was unemployed it just meant that he had not gone far enough west. In the agrarian-based, self-sufficient, economy of much of the country, the concept of *unemployment* made little sense. One stayed busy providing for oneself and one's family. Carving farms out of the countryside provided more than a lifetime's work for the entire family from children who could toddle — they could feed the animals — to the elderly, who could cook, spin yarn(s), and whittle.

The idea of being integrated into an exchange system, buying and selling goods and one's own labor, was not widespread. Population density was minimal and it might be days between seeing a 'neighbor'. Some people chose farming precisely to avoid the commercialization of life. They avoided towns and certainly cities. Moves westward into less populated areas suited them and this attitude was still prevalent on the prairies in the late 1800s.[61]

Raw land? Move? Is that it? Where was the government's social safety-net? In 1800 the federal government spending was about 2% of GDP, or $24/person <u>per year</u> (slightly more than $2 per person per month) in 2011 dollars. In 1820, its presence had risen to about 3% of GDP, spending per person rose to $33.20 (2011 dollars) annually. At the start of the Civil War, federal government spending had fallen back to 2.3% of GDP, during the war this rose to 13%, but by the late 1870s it had fallen back to about 3%, with spending person about $139 in 1880.[62^63]

---

[59] 1967 = 100. If one extends the post-Civil war period to the mid-1870s the price level drop is even more pronounced; dropping to 32 by 1876. All data from: www.minneapolisfed.org/community_education/teacher/calc/hist1800.cfm[59] Israel (1998), pps. 16-21.

[60] Josephsen (1959), pps. 64-65.

[61] Mayhew (1972).

[62^63] Again, in 2011 dollars. As a comparison, today (2011) Federal government expenditures are about 25% of GDP and are approximately $12,100 per person. This is some 500 times what they were in 1800 and about 90 times what they were in 1880, *per person.*

People looking for assistance looked within their families and local neighborhoods. The federal government beyond the post office was rather hard to find. The small federal government presence in post-war economies shrank back towards pre-war levels, limited as it was by philosophy and by the small revenue derived from customs duties and tariffs.

What Edison could see running this simplified system on his test bench is that a generalized inflation or deflation of the price level was highly unlikely unless there were something, like wars, to gum up the mechanism. What else might be sand in the gears?

Having dealt with some of the country's most noted financiers, and having a grudging respect for them, Edison also knew that markets could be manipulated if someone (or group) had market power. If a market was monopolized, or 'cornered', the price in that market would rise. But, cornering one market does not raise enough prices to raise the price level or index. But, what if the cornered market affects *all* the other markets?

In the gold standard, gold is the good that affects all other markets. Edison saw that if someone cornered the gold market they could restrict the supply of gold, raise its price in terms of goods and services (prices of goods would *fall* relative to gold), and make monopoly profits for themselves. Their gold will buy more than it should. People selling goods and services will get less gold than they should.

Skeptical and cautious as he was, Edison did not think that this simple model with a monopolized gold market grafted on to 'explain' the 1920-1921 deflation, really applied to the modern system in which he lived. If someone cornered the gold market in the U.S., and gold prices rose (goods prices fall), wouldn't gold flow in from abroad in search of low-priced bargains? Then, doesn't the gold price fall again in the U.S.?

It would be hard to monopolize the world gold market. How many gold mines were there in the world? How easy was it to keep prospectors from going to the four corners of the world to search out more gold? To corner any market takes coordination and control powers that may be applied to a particular good, but are impractical when discussing something like gold. If its price rises, anyone—anywhere in the world can go look for more of it. Poof! The monopoly evaporates.

Monopolize gold? In Edison's experience even having the legal right — a patent — to monopolize a single good (that could not be dug out of the ground by just anyone) did not guarantee control. He sadly noted that a patent is "simply an invitation to a lawsuit" and imitators.[64] If he spent years chasing copycats through the courts, over thirty years

[64] Quoted in Josephson (1959), page 355.

on one case alone!, how easy would it be for anyone to control the gold market?

Yet, as we saw above, he railed against some in the financial system. What is the simple story above — the simple test-bench financial model — missing? A banking system! In the test-bench model, gold is circulating for goods, anyone can find it in the ground, it flows freely across markets and borders. If one needed more gold, one either grabbed a pickaxe and hoped to get lucky or made something and sold it for gold. Did people actually *do* that? Did gold actually circulate? Edison most often saw paper notes, paper money, not gold, circulating. These notes were printed and issued by banks not dug out of the ground. Does this make a difference? Including banks will make his test model more realistic at the expense of increasing the level of complexity. He started to see why analyzing the problem was so demanding.

Back to the test bench. To understand the banking sector Edison asked himself: 'Why banks?' His personal experience with banks and bankers had been rocky at best leading to his low opinion of most bankers.[65] But, he knew if he was going to make progress on the 'money complex' he was going to have to forget his distaste of bankers at the test bench. Electricity could kill you faster than a banker, but that did not mean you avoided it in the lab.

He also knew that most people liked and trusted their local bankers; however, they were suspicious of big city banks. In Alabama he railed against:

> "the money brokers, the money profiteers, the private bankers' who "gain their power through a fictitious and false value given to gold."

but the commercial banks — the ones on your dusty town's street corners — were expressly absolved:

> "Make it perfectly clear that I'm not advocating any changes in banks and banking. Banks are a mighty good thing. They are essential to the commerce of the country."[66]

Going back to the founding of the country, individual states chartered banks and they usually did not limit the number.[67] By the time Edison was investigating, there were over twenty-nine *thousand* banks in the U.S. These banks took deposits and made loans. If you

---

[65] Money "brokers" operate a bit differently than bankers, but they fulfill most of the same functions. They both are intermediaries, making the borrowing-lending process easier and lower cost; brokers do it by matching lenders and borrowers for a fee. Edison thought they were part of the scheme that caused gold to be over-valued, to their benefit.

[66] *New York Times*, Dec. 6, 1921, page 6.

[67] A charter is the legal authority to engage in the business. It's like a license to be a banker.

had gold, they were a reasonably safe repository. They built impressive buildings and vaults to prove their care and concern for your gold. In return for your gold they either gave you a checking deposit or their paper money (paper bank notes) representing the value of the gold. You either spent the money, or, when you wanted the gold back you brought the paper money back and exchanged it for the gold. The issuing bank had to accept their paper notes in exchange for gold.

Your incentive is a safe place for your gold and the ease and convenience of using a check or paper money instead of clunky gold coins in transactions. The banker's incentive is to use your gold to increase the bank's income. To induce you to deposit your gold, the banker gives you convenient, lightweight, paper notes redeemable at the bank for the gold you have deposited.[68] These are a gold receipt and you can spend them where ever they are recognized and accepted. If the bank has a good reputation, they are as 'good as gold'.

What does the banker do with your gold? If he could only print the same value of paper notes as he held of your gold, then there was no way for him to use your gold beyond, perhaps, charging you a storage fee for safe-keeping. He would have to hold it until the bank's paper notes return to redeem it. This looks no different than the gold standard we explored above, except that paper notes circulate instead of (or perhaps, along side) gold. Yet, a paper note requires gold to back it. To get more paper dollars someone has to find more gold.

The international result remains the same. If prices rise in the U.S. relative to those in a foreign country, paper dollars are redeemed for gold, gold flows out buying foreign currency (pounds, pesos, yen, or whatever), the foreign currency is used to buy the cheaper foreign goods. In the end, gold flows out of the U.S. and to the foreign country. Goods flow from the foreign country to the U.S. Ultimately, the price levels are re-equilibrated as they were above in the gold-circulating case.[69]

Real banks have more options. States allowed banks to print more paper notes than the value of the gold they held. Called *fractional-reserve* banking, it allows bankers to create new — and identical — paper notes to loan out at interest. If the borrower makes his principal

---

[68] In what follows assume that the banker issues paper notes instead of creating checking deposits. It does not make a difference to the story, but it is simpler to do one or the other.

[69] Countries typically fixed their currency to a specific weight of gold of a specific purity; in this way, the currencies were fixed against each other. The U.S. Gold Standard Act of 1900 fixed the value of a dollar at 25⁸⁄₁₀ grains of gold at 90% purity, equivalent to 23.22 grains (1.5046 grams) of pure gold; this meant gold had a value of just over $20.67 per Troy ounce. England fixed its 'pound sterling' (£) at 113 grains of gold. These rates imply a rate of $4.87=£1.

and interest payments the banker makes an income and you, the owner of the gold — holding the first batch of paper dollars — is none the wiser.

Let's all be bankers and print a boatload of dollar notes! Can it be that easy? Is a bank charter a license to print money? The loan process involves the banker printing those new paper dollars, giving them to the borrower, and then hoping for two things. First, that the borrower makes the principal and interest payments; and second, that the paper dollars returning to the bank for redemption at any given time do not have greater value than the gold in the vault.

If you deposit $10 in gold and receive $10 in paper notes, your bank has 100% in gold reserves against the paper notes issued. If a paper dollar comes back to the bank for redemption into gold, the banker has it covered. If your bank attracts a borrower and gives him a $10 loan in paper notes, your bank now has $20 in paper notes circulating and only $10 in gold 'backing' it. Its reserves of $10 in gold are only 50% against its $20 circulating paper money liabilities. Your banker is taking the risk that at some point, more than $10 in paper notes will appear for redemption and he will not have enough gold to redeem them all. This would be catastrophic for the bank as no one willingly places their gold in a bank that cannot redeem it. The bank and banker would lose credibility and probably have to shut its doors.

Look what fractional reserve banking means for the tight connection between gold, money, and prices. Instead of a direct connection between the volume of gold and paper dollars, as in the simple banking model, fractional-reserve banking creates some slippage in the system. The process is no longer automatic. It depends on the banker's desire and willingness to issue or retire paper notes.

If the quantity of paper dollars increases, prices rise and so does the price index. Inflation. If the quantity of paper dollars decreases, prices fall, and so does the price index. Deflation.

In an example on the following pages, banks use gold as a fulcrum to back the paper money supply pushing down on the 'lever' creating an 'extra' supply of paper money. Each paper dollar is backed by 2/3 of a dollar in gold. The bankers are willing to have $3 in paper money outstanding for each $2 in gold they have in the vault. Total money supply rises by 50 percent and the price level rises from P=100 to P=150.

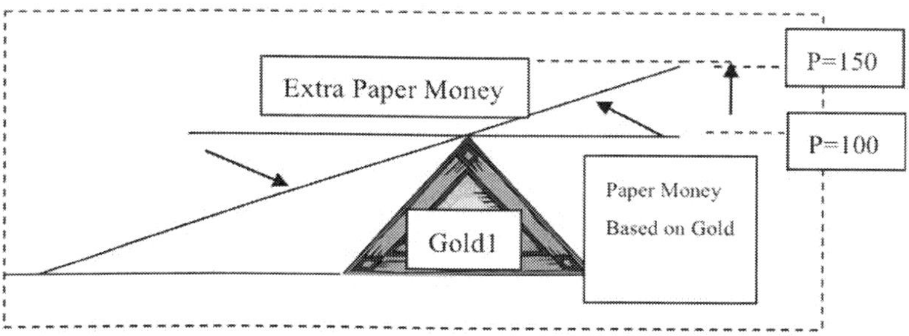

What limits the number of paper notes a bank will create? Imagine bankers are risk-takers and grant every loan in search of more interest income? Could a very small amount of actual metal in the vault be backing a larger and larger number of circulating bank notes? If so, would inflation, as Edison had seen it, result?

Didn't Archimedes say: "Give me a fulcrum and a long enough lever and I can move the world?" Give bankers a golden fulcrum and the 'profit lever', they can move the price level. If bankers decided to be stricter about making loans, not printing as many new dollars, or even 'calling in' loans, would that lead to deflation?

If bankers are willing to risk having only $1 in gold backing for every $2 in paper dollars, then they push down harder on the 'lever' and up goes the price level to 200 for a given amount of gold.

Banks use gold as a fulcrum to back the paper money supply creating an even greater 'extra' supply of paper money, the total money supply rises by 100 percent and the price level rises from P=100 to P=200.

From the perspective of an individual banker — one of 29,000 — being the cause of a nation's inflation or deflation was unthinkable.

Each bank is typically small and the number of its bank notes very small relative to the total. If every banker thought this way, extending more loans and printing more bank notes would make sense. Why not print an infinite number of paper notes? If inflation resulted, well, that was the fault of all the others, not one little bank. The limit on note creation would be the individual banker's fear of bank-note redemption before loan repayment. Banks must balance their desire for additional interest income from more loans against the devastation of a redemption crunch.[70]

There is also the international 'governor' limiting paper note creation. If the banks in the United States print more dollars leading to rising prices, then bargain hunters in the United States will buy foreign goods, redeeming their paper dollars for gold, using the gold to pur-

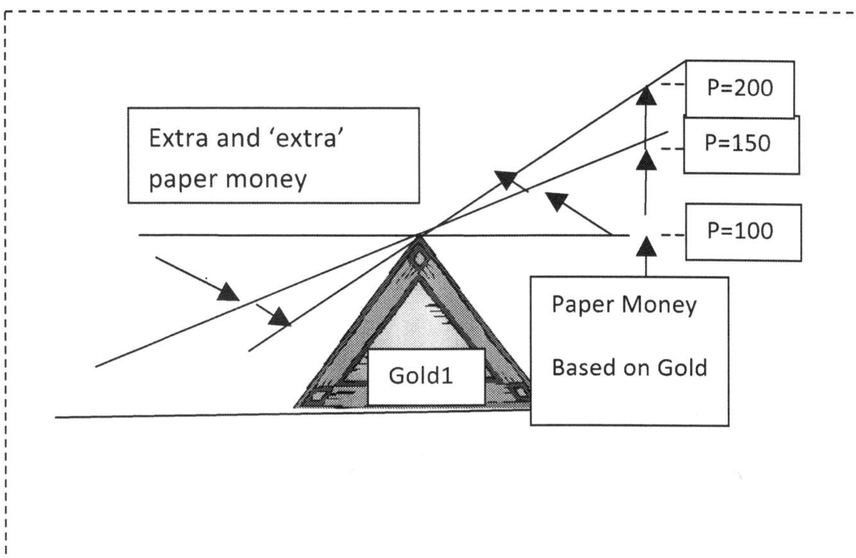

chase foreign currency and the gold supply — and paper money supply — declines in the U.S, ending the inflation. This action does raise the gold and paper money supply in the foreign country, leading to higher prices for foreigners. They may blame the U.S. for 'exporting' its inflation. However, if United States. banks stop printing the new dollars as

[70] Banks would also have to worry about the probability of repayment, known as default risk. In boom times banks tend to create more loans because the probability of being repaid looks more promising. In 'bust' times, loans are very hard to get as banks fear rising default levels. This mechanism adds a "pro-cyclical" element to banking — tending to over-boost the good times and be overly constraining in the bad times.

gold flows out, prices have to equalize, perhaps at a new higher level, worldwide.[71]

Aha! Edison thought he'd found the culprit. Not all banks were created equal. Sure, there were thousands of them, but some were much larger than others. The smaller ones often borrowed from the larger ones. The more they could borrow, the more loans they could make in their communities.[72] That would increase their income and increase local business activity. Boom times! However, if the larger banks wanted their gold back, they would call in those loans. These smaller banks would have to deliver gold (or the larger bank's paper dollars) and that would 'crunch' the smaller banks, their 'golden pyramids' would shrink. They would have to call in loans from their borrowers. Business activity in their towns would shrink. Depression.

Business on some Main Streets *was* a hostage to the whims of the larger banks, the 'Wall Streeters'. That's how it looked to Edison and people in the small towns across the country. Even if one did not believe that the 'money brokers' or big Wall Street banks had cornered the gold-based currency markets, it looked as if they caused much grief by lumbering, ignorantly if not malevolently, through the economy. Was anyone looking at them? Where was their Sherman Antitrust Act?[73]

---

[71] You may be thinking that you have never bought anything from abroad — but the stores you go to send their buyers around the world looking for bargains. Those goods appear on your stores' shelves and you may buy them. So, indirectly, you *do* buy from abroad.

[72] In addition to branching restrictions, Larger banks did not enter every small town market due to cost and scale considerations. The larger banks in the cities did not know where the little borrowers in the towns were, but it was in their interest to know where the small town banks were. This is before the internet—heck, it's almost before the telephone.

[73] According to Israel (1998), page 446, Edison considered the Sherman Antitrust Act of 1890 unscientific, inexpertly written and applied by lawyers who knew nothing of business and made no effort to consult experts before implementing it. He would not make the same mistake in his money researches.

CHAPTER 5: INTEREST AND THE CENTRAL BANK

Considering government involvement in banking and interest meant adding one more layer to the test bench model representing the financial system of the 1920s.

In response to the potential problems of paper money 'over-issue', exporting inflation, whipsaws, trust issues, and other banking concerns, the U.S. and most other countries had a government-chartered agency or bank responsible for managing the banking system and overall supply of bank notes. This bank, referred to as a *central bank* often started as a private bank in competition with other banks. Under a gold standard its notes also circulated and were redeemable for gold.

The central bank was not always the sole issuer of paper currency, but it usually had supervisory and regulatory powers that other banks did not have.[74] The central bank also could play the important role of *lender of last resort.* This allows a crucial disconnect from the Wall Streeters and Main Streeters. Even if Wall Street tightened and demanded repayment, if the Main Street bank could go to the central bank for a loan, they did not have to call in their loans from local businesses. Therefore, the Wall Street move would not automatically result in a depression in outer regions served by smaller banks.

If it really worked this way, where was the problem? Was the current recession a mirage? Why was Edison test-benching any of this? What sort of central bank did the U.S. have, why, and who ran it?

Central banking was at the heart of many debates in the U.S. in the late 1780s. Alexander Hamilton, who saw a coming industrialization and business-oriented country growing out of the revolution, argued for a strong central bank. Thomas Jefferson, who believed that tilling the soil and a large degree of self-sufficiency were in the nation's future, countered that small, state banks would be sufficient to handle the limited trading needs of the agrarian populace. Compromising in 1791, Congress granted a twenty-year charter to the owners of the First Bank of the United States and subscribed to twenty percent ownership. Located in Philadelphia, as well as being a bank it was the fiscal agent for the young federal government. The charter expired without renewal in 1811.

In 1816, Congress granted the Second Bank of the United States also located in Philadelphia, a twenty-year charter. Again, with

---

[74] These might include a national reserve-requirement ratio, the types of assets a bank could hold, restrictions on the types of loans it made, the amount of owner's equity — paid-in capital — it held relative to assets, and other restrictions.

twenty percent Federal government ownership, this bank branched throughout the growing country and took a more active role in financing national economic activity.[75] Given its size and importance, after all the U.S. government banked there, it soon saw itself — and was seen as — the nation's bank.

Fueling a land boom it loaned liberally upon receiving its charter in 1816. By 1818 bank managers tightened lending, interest rates rose, land prices fell, production dropped resulting in the Panic of 1819. This is an inflation-deflation episode where the volume of gold may not have changed, but the fluctuation in bank notes caused a price bubble, excessive lending and borrowing, defaults, and a bursting bubble. By raising interest rates, the Second Bank may have put its private interest above the public good. That's how it looked to those who could not make their payments and lost their farms.

The Second Bank was also accused of playing unfairly in forcing note redemption at smaller, competing state banks. It presented state bank notes for redemption into gold. This depleted the gold that these banks had for lending. Their loans and income fell. Business activity collapsed. Gold went to the 'big city' Second Bank which was then in a stronger position to make loans and its income rose. Many of the smaller banks, in the 'country' of the south and west[76], closed as the gold flowed out.

The resulting bank failures created a financial panic and depression. It was like losing gold and prices dropped in that region. While falling prices sound good to the consumer they go hand in hand with a rising value of money meaning a rising burden of debt. Borrowers — debtors — are made much worse off. Given that most people in the agrarian south and west were debtors, those regions were especially hard hit.

Capitalizing on the rising tide of anger aimed at the big city bank and bankers, holding the loans the rural folk owed, Andrew Jackson launched successful campaigns for the Presidency in 1828 and

[75] As a condition of their charter, state banks were prohibited from branching across state lines. Sometime the prohibition limited them to one storefront, sometime limited them to their headquarters city, a county or, the state as a whole. The geographic restriction within state differed state by state, but typically it ensured that these banks would remain small.

[76] In 1820 the deep "southern" states were Louisiana, Mississippi, Alabama, Georgia and the "western" states included Missouri (sort of, admitted to statehood in 1821), Illinois, Indiana, Tennessee, and Kentucky. Though the latter two also had 'eastern' portions. But, the reader hopefully gets the idea that "western" interest in 1820 covered a vastly different region of the country than it does in the early twenty-first century.

1832. Once in office, he vetoed re-chartering the Second Bank.[77] That was the end of 'central' banking in the U.S. until 1913.

Edison was reading late into the night — 'burning the midnight oil' — as he wrote to more than one correspondent. During the Civil War both governments had difficulty financing their war efforts turning to printing paper currency as a financing tool. The Federal government suspended the conversion of its newly issued paper notes — 'greenbacks' — into gold, sparking fears of inflation and giving birth to the epithet: "greenbackism" meaning *wildly inflationary*. As we saw above, during the war, inflation did reach 80% in the north, over 9000% in the south, which used the printing press more freely. Protecting their gold holdings, some major banks also suspended convertibility of their bank notes.

After the Civil War, the nation experienced several financial panics with the most severe being those of 1873, 1893, and 1907. A financial panic features some or all of: rapidly rising prices of some key assets — e.g., a 'tech' or housing bubble. Then, 'Pop!', a slowing of the price increases or even rapidly falling price, a loss of confidence in values, credit market dislocation, lenders are very cautious in lending, rising interest rates, continued falling prices now more widespread as economic activity slows, rising uncertainty and pessimism, loan defaults, bankruptcies, runs on banks as people withdraw their gold, bank failures, and quickly rising unemployment. There are sometimes different features in each panic. In 1893, for example, exacerbating the panic were widespread droughts in the Midwest making the farmers' plight even more difficult.

The panics of 1873 and 1893 were associated with a technology boom, the new, innovative technology being railroads and associated technology like telegraphy to which Edison was making innovative contributions. Massive investments in track and facilities, opened new territory and drove up land speculation and real estate prices. Much of the investment in the railroads came from England and Europe. When over-building occurred and some large companies defaulted on their loans, banks failed. Fear of more bank failures caused bank runs by depositors. They withdrew their gold if they could. This caused more banks to fail.

[77]As president, Jackson oversaw the withdrawal of the government's accounts from the bank — net deposit outflow — and deposited them (deposit inflow) — in several state banks. This hastened the bank's financial failure. Jackson also won the popular vote in the presidential election of 1824, but lost to John Quincy Adams in the House of Representatives. Given his adamant opposition to the Second Bank and his belief that it acted to choke economic activity in the south and west, it is ironic that Jackson's image is on the $20 Federal Reserve note today.

With the bursting of the railroad 'bubble', land prices fell and the farmer's asset — land — now was worth less than when they borrowed to buy it. We would say that they were "upside down" or "under water" on their loans. Many defaulted. That created more distrust of lenders — bankers — and more disruption in banking.

Edison remembered these panics well. In 1873 and 1874 he was actively seeking financial backing for his work on telegraphy. In 1873, as well as loans being difficult to get, his tight financial situation meant giving up the family house and moving in to a small, second floor, apartment over a store. In 1893, falling prices meant difficulty in meeting his payments, juggling creditors, even suspending cash payments to his workers.[78]

The panic of 1907 threatened to shake the New York financial system to its core. It was no better for Edison. His phonograph business was "hard hit".[79] Blamed on financial speculation in New York, the financial panic spread throughout the country as banks and businesses failed leading to deflation and higher unemployment nationwide. This episode was viewed as 'the nation' paying for the excesses of a greedy few in New York causing the collapse by speculation and insider deal making. The nation — and Congress — were pointing the finger and it pointed right at Wall Street.[80]

Congress wanted to find the culprits and fix the monetary system to end 'panics'. The National Monetary Commission was formed in 1908 and staffed with experts to recommend solutions. The Commission recommended the creation of a 'reserve association' that would step in and provide an *elastic currency* being a *lender of last resort* for banks undergoing rapid gold loss. It concluded that a 'bank for banks' would provide a place for the local bank to get the short-term loan needed to prevent bank collapse and panics.

In late 1913, the Federal Reserve System, the central bank in the U.S. was created.[81] Edison believed it was the 'greatest thing accomplished in the U.S. in 1913'.

> "President Wilson deserves a lot of credit. He has taken a step in the right direction. We must get rid of this terrible money evil. We don't want everything controlled by a few in this country…".[82]

---

[78] Israel (1998), pages 100, 354.

[79] Josephson (1959), page 418.

[80] That it was a Wall Street banker, J.P. Morgan, who rescued the federal government in 1893 and led the rescue mission on Wall Street in the Panic of 1907 only made skeptics even more worried about the big city (New York) bankers. Morgan was also one of Edison's early investors.

[81] The Federal Reserve Act was signed in to law December 23, 1913. The Federal Reserve System is often referred to as "the Fed".

[82] *New York Times*, February 12, 1914, page 1.

The Fed's structure reflects the many long-standing concerns in American banking. These include: the distrust of the 'big city' (e.g. "Wall Street") private bankers and brokers, distrust of government control of money, regionalism, and a fear that the 'little guy' ("Main Streeter") is being ignored, or worse, getting her pockets picked and played for a sucker. The Federal Reserve System was created to disperse and diffuse financial power, serve all of the country equally, and be both privately and publicly owned and directed.

In this period, busy with the phonograph, movies, and the new conglomerate, *Thomas A. Edison, Inc.*, Edison was not paying much attention to the goings on in Washington. But, now on the test bench, Edison saw how the Federal Reserve was designed to augment and control the existing banking system.

The Federal Reserve Act created twelve Federal Reserve districts across the country with associated headquarters banks.[83] Owned by their member commercial (Main Street) banks their leadership comes from their regional district.[84] The Reserve banks are responsible for lending to banks in their district. Banks would approach them for a short term loan when they feared a gold outflow which could not be more easily handled e.g., by calling in a loan or selling an asset like a bond.

While the mechanism worked a bit differently, think of these Federal Reserve Banks printing new paper currency notes, backed by gold just like all bank notes, and handing them to the bankers. The bankers used their commercial loans to local businesses as collateral for the loan from the Fed. The Reserve Bank charged interest, *the discount rate,* and movements in that rate moderated a bank's enthusiasm for obtaining a loan from the Fed. A lower rate made loans from the Reserve Bank less costly; a higher rate made borrowing more costly.[85]

The important part this played in the financial system was that now there was a Reserve Bank in every district, familiar with local conditions. Each of these banks stood ready to lend to help a member

---

[83] See Hammes (2001), for more on how the districts and cities were chosen. The populists led by Bryan, wanted forty-eight (one in each state) Reserve Banks.

[84] Nationally chartered banks were required to become members of the System and become part owners of these Reserve banks. State chartered banks could choose to become members or stay out of the System. Being a member allowed a bank the right to the Federal Reserve's lending window, known as the *discount window*. Non-members did not have this right.

[85] Altering the level and growth rate of the money supply, changing the reserve requirement, and changing the discount rate is known as *monetary policy*. It is what central banks are responsible for — in this case the Federal Reserve System. Note, in the early days, with some regional isolation, each Reserve Bank could have a slightly different monetary policy.

bank. The money brokers could not hold small banks and regions hostage to their demands. The Fed provided an alternative, an *elastic currency,* one stretching with the needs of business activity.[86]

The hope was this would prevent the inter-regional cascading of financial hardship which featured prominently in panics. Now, a small bank facing outflows, could go to their Federal Reserve Bank and cover that outflow. They did not have to withdraw their gold from a correspondent bank in another city. They did not have to call in loans, they did not have to sell assets, sometime at a 'fire sale' price. A financial problem could be contained, localized, and not have far-reaching effects whirling into a full-blown panic.

This system did not supplant private banking, it added a *bank for banks.* It also provided a national-level supervisor and regulator of member commercial banks.[87] At the top, giving counsel, advice and overseeing matters, the five-member board in Washington D.C., appointed by the U.S. president was intended to represent the public interest. This would disperse private banking power and prevent the big city (i.e. Wall Street) bankers from running amok.

If central banks did their jobs well, domestic financial panics would be limited, of short duration, and contained within their region. There would be no financial instability to export or import. In times of international distress, central banks could coordinate policies, even to the extent of borrowing and lending to and from each other.

Central banks overlay the financial system. They had and have immense power. They could change the fraction of gold banks had to hold against paper notes. By changing their lending rates they could make it easier or harder for commercial banks to make loans to their customers. If a 'money broker' or a banker tried to take advantage of a small bank, the central bank could step in and be the lender. In times of distress, they could ameliorate a panic. On the other hand, if they raised lending rates, it was the same as if they were taking gold away from banks. A central bank exercised a great deal of power over the entire

[86] See Meltzer (2003), chapters 1 and 2. These discount loans were to be made with relatively short-term, industrial or goods-based, business loans as collateral. Initially, farm loans were not considered to be of high enough quality — plus they tended to be too long-term — to be used as collateral for a loan from the Fed.

[87] While all nationally chartered banks had to become members, it was an option for state chartered banks. Criteria they had to assess were the added regulatory costs, like the initial payment for ownership and higher legal reserve requirements, imposed by the Reserve Bank. Against these higher costs they had to consider the advantages of having a lender of last resort. Not all state chartered banks chose membership. If a bank was not a member, it could not apply to the Fed for a short-term loan, no matter what sort of collateral it held. This is why most bank failures were not member banks of the System. This changed in 1980.

system. It had the power to take money out of the hands of business people, power to destroy jobs, power to starve innovators.

Edison shook his head. "I am studying economics intensively," he wrote, "especially money. The subject is intricate but I am going to stick."[88] After modeling the system on his test bench, Edison was even more convinced in 1922 that the underlying problem was "...due to a bad system of money...the very poor supervision over the actions of banks..." and that "...an artificial scarcity is maintained by those who use gold to monopolize money."

Now he knew how the money system worked, from simple to complex. At the top, responsible for the system of money and the supervision of banks, the central bank, the Fed. Edison, a supporter of the Fed, wondered, what did they do during the war? Though signed in to law in December 1913, the Fed did not actually come on-line until late 1914. It took time to figure out where to site the Reserve Banks, develop operating policies, hire people, and get a large system like this grafted on to the financial system. The war started before the opening of the Reserve District banks.

Designed to be an independent agency, wartime exigencies meant their independence was sacrificed to maintain interest rates that lowered the Treasury's cost of wartime borrowing. The Treasury needed to borrow to finance the war and low interest rates were good for borrowers. The Fed became "subservient to the Treasury's perceived needs."[89] The Federal Reserve's discount rate fell from 6% in 1914 to a low of 3%, which it maintained through 1917, and then 4%, which it maintained through 1919. The discount rate is the cost of funds to commercial banks, the lower it is (relative to the general level of interest rates) the more 'expansive' the Fed is and the easier borrowing is. If the discount rate rises borrowing costs rise and there is less borrowing.

Partially in response to the accommodative wartime financing, the money supply — the paper dollars — doubled from mid-1914 to mid-1919.[90] Price inflation resulted. In response to the price inflation and as a signal that the Fed was establishing a semblance of independence from the Treasury, the New York Fed raised its discount rate in three steps from 4% to 7% through the first half of 1920. Monetary contraction — fewer paper dollars — and deflation followed.

---

[88] To H.J. Blumhart, Adair, Iowa, April 5, 1922. TENHP Banking 1922.

[89] Meltzer, op cit, page 85.

[90] Friedman and Schwartz, 1963, Table A-1, page 708 and 709. Though, as their discussion, pages 208-213, makes evident, this was primarily a 'gold inflation', gold flows to the U.S. could not be sterilized — or neutralized — by the Federal Reserve. The low level of government debt outstanding meant that there was virtually no market in "treasuries", nor could the Fed issue its own debt in order to reduce the money stock.

The deflation was the result of central banks' goals. The New York Fed's governor, Benjamin Strong, and Montague Norman of Great Britain's central bank, the Bank of England, had the goal of returning their country's currency-to-gold exchange rates to their pre-war rates.[91]

Edison concluded that the war and the Fed's inexperience created the 1916-1922 boom-bust whipsaw. During the war gold flowed in to the U.S. and the Fed lowered interest rates making loans easier for banks. These changes created inflation. Then the Fed's desire to 'return to normalcy' (pre-war currency exchange rates) caused it to raise interest rates. Loans dried up. Deflation.

By the end of World War One, the conventional wisdom — based on the nineteenth-century experiences — was that the economic hothouse bubble created by wartime exigencies and financing would be met with a significant post-war slump. Despite the existence of a network of central banks, including the Fed, the view of the nation's bankers was not much changed from the nineteenth-century view of their grandfathers. Painfully popping bubbles and busts always followed inflating wartime bubbles. No less an authority than the nation's top banker, the New York Fed's governor, Benjamin Strong, said so. Strong —

> "...a proponent of fixed exchange rates and the gold standard... accepted deflation when required and came to regard it as the price of international stability."[92]

— was ready as a matter of necessity for the post-war economy to endure deflation.

> "Strong replied that the deflation was an inevitable consequence of the previous inflation: 'No one could have stopped it, and no one could have started it. In our opinion, it was bound to come.' "[93]

> Strong knew there were real costs of deflation. He predicted the deflation would be 'accompanied by a considerable degree of unemployment, but not for very long, and that after a year or two of discomfort, embarrassment, some losses, some disorders caused by unemployment, we will emerge with an almost invincible banking position, prices more nearly at competitive levels with other nations...' ".[94]

---

[91] Meltzer (2003), pps. 110 and 111; footnote 90, also cites Keynes' at-the-time support for this return to the gold standard at pre-war parities.

[92] Meltzer, 2003, page 75.

[93] Meltzer, Op. cit., page 114.

[94] Meltzer, op cit., page 110. The internal quote is from Strong's letter to the economist Edwin Kemmerer, February 1919. The phrase "after a year or two of..." evokes Keynes' famous riposte, "The long run is a misleading guide to current affairs. In the long run we are all dead." See Keynes (1923), pg. 65.

The Farm Products and All Commodities price indexes for the period give graphic views of the whipsaw:

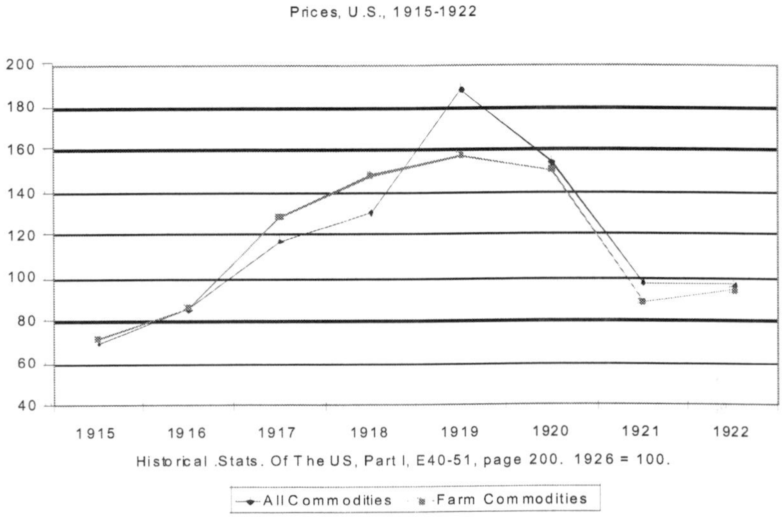

Prices more than doubled from 1915 to 1919 and then fell by about 40% to 50% in two years. If Benjamin Strong was ready to accept the 'inevitability' of this whipsaw and its consequent impact on employment and losses, Edison and others were not.

Edison's time at the test bench was paying off. He was convinced that he saw the problem. Despite there being a central bank, if they acted according to the (g)old laws, the (g)old way of thinking, the (g)old system, why, one got the (g)old results. This made him think that: "…a great many persons seem to be in a rut and their minds refuse to act…".[95]

He thought he understood the money complex and he saw that he still had work to do. That critic, Henry Hazlitt, had suggested a book. Edison was going to keep studying and he was going to get these people out of their rut and get the country running again.

[95] To Irving Fisher, August 7, 1922. TENHP Banking 1922.

CHAPTER 6: IS HISTORY BUNK—OR CAN WE LEARN FROM IT?

"I am studying Economics intensively, especially money. The subject is intricate, but I am going to stick."[96]

Stung and chastened by Henry Hazlitt's criticism that he was ignorant of the monetary issues and history, Edison directed his assistant to 'Get that book!' The book was Andrew D. White's provocatively titled: *Fiat Money Inflation in France.*[97] Edison would not come off looking unprepared again, he wanted to be: "put right in order that I may make no statements which...would be found to be incorrect."

He started reading White's short book. It was a shocking story of good intentions gone awry with devastating consequences for the eighteenth-century French public.

The French experiment with irredeemable paper money in 1790 was a surprise given the recent debacle surrounding John Law's scheme that started so well in 1716, but left the country impoverished by mid-1720. Were memories so short? Had they forgotten the eerily familiar beginnings of the plan? In both periods, the country in depression, a government deeply in debt, the capacity for more taxation exhausted. In its final months, Law's paper money scheme featured an inflation rate of 23% per month.[98]

How would the Assembly of 1790, faced with large budget deficits, large debt, and similar tax 'exhaustion', design a paper currency that would not inflate prices when the clever Law failed so spectacularly?

Many of the French legislators of the day asked these same questions, some even waving pieces of Law's money in the air exclaiming: "that it was stained with the blood and tears of their fathers."[99] Nor should we assume that the legislators of the day were ignorant, wild-eyed, revolutionaries, as White wrote:

---

[96] Notes from Edison to H.J. Blumhart, Adair, IA, April 5, 1922. Letter in Banking 1922, TENHP.

[97] *Fiat* is Latin for law. Thus fiat money is "money by law". White (1832-1918) was the first president of Cornell University after experience as a diplomat, professor of history and English literature at the University of Michigan, and as a New York State legislator. There he and Ezra Cornell developed the idea for a new land-grant university in New York state on Cornell's farm.

[98] Moen, J. (2001), "John Law and the Mississippi Bubble: 1718-1720." *Mississippi History Now*, online at: http://mshistory.k12.ms.us/articles/70/john-law-and-the-mississippi-bubble-1718-1720; accessed May 30, 2010.

[99] White, A.D., (1896, 1933), page 6.

"...no inference could be more wide of the fact. Whatever may have been the character of the men who legislated for France afterward, no thoughtful student of history can deny...that few more keen-sighted legislative bodies have met than this first French Constitutional Assembly...But the current toward paper money had become irresistible. It was constantly urged, and with a great show of force, that if any nation could safely issue it, France was now that nation; that she was fully warned by her severe experience under John Law; that she was now a constitutional government, controlled by an enlightened, patriotic people — not, as in the days of the former issues of paper money, an absolute monarchy controlled by politicians and adventurers; that she was able to secure every *livre* of her paper money by a virtual mortgage on a landed domain vastly greater in value than the entire issue; that, with men like Bailly, Mirabeau and Necker at her head, she could not commit the financial mistakes and crimes from which France had suffered under John Law, the Regent Duke of Orleans and Cardinal Dubois."[100]

The French *assignats* were supposedly backed by French lands and were to bear interest. At first the economy rebounded smartly. The government paid down its debt with the newly issued currency, credit revived, "trade increased and all difficulties seemed to vanish."[101] As the government succumbed to the ease of paying its costs by printing and issuing more *assignats,* great inflationary pressures built. The government tried to control this pressure by legislating prices, imposing heavy fines, and even imposing the death penalty for those selling the currency at a discount. The combination of inflation and price controls led to food shortages. Riots and great social unrest ensued. Stability was only re-established by Napoleon's ascendance and a new currency.

From inception in 1790 to 1795, the 35-fold increase in *assignats* generated an exponentially rising inflation with the price level rising by well over 100-fold. One 'dollar' shrunk down below one penny in purchasing power. Inflation wiped out savings and impoverished the average citizen. [102]

Edison could not have missed White's message; to reinforce it White drew parallels of calls in the 1870s U.S. for 'more money':

"I am sure that it never occurred, either to my Michigan students [between 1858 and 1863] or to myself, that it could ever have any bearing on our own country. It certainly never entered into our minds that any such folly as that exhibited in those French documents of the eighteenth century could ever find supporters in the United States of the nineteenth.

Some years later, when there began to be demands for large issues of paper money in the United States, I wrought some of the facts thus collected into a speech in the Senate of the State of New York, showing the need of especial care in such dealings with financial necessities.

---

[100] Ibid pages 6-7.
[101] Ibid. page 10.
[102] Ibid, page 26.

In 1876, during the "greenback craze," General Garfield and Mr. S. B. Crittenden, both members of the House of Representatives at that time, asked me to read a paper on the same general subject before an audience of Senators and Representatives of both parties in Washington. This I did, and also gave it later before an assemblage of men of business at the Union League Club in New York.

Various editions of the paper were afterward published, among them, two or three for campaign purposes, in the hope that they might be of use in showing to what folly, cruelty, wrong and pain the passion for "fiat money" may lead.

Other editions were issued at a later period, in view of the principle involved in the proposed unlimited coinage of silver in the United States, which was, at bottom, the idea which led to that fearful wreck of public and private prosperity in France.

For these editions there was an added reason in the fact that the utterances of sundry politicians at that time pointed clearly to issues of paper money practically unlimited. These men were logical enough to see that it would be inconsistent to stop at the unlimited issue of silver dollars which cost really something when they could issue unlimited paper dollars which virtually cost nothing."[103]

White carefully illustrated that in the best of all possible circumstances, a "fiat money" whose issue is unchecked, would inevitably lead to ruin. Not just economic ruin, but social and political ruin, as well. White carefully shows that 1790s France was not being governed by a despot, bent upon raising his personal glory and wealth at the expense of the commoners. France of 1790 was governed by those who remembered history, were intelligent, enlightened, and were the best minds of their time.

Yet, when managing paper money, they blew it. John Law had blown it before them. Recent experience in the U.S. Civil War showed that it did not matter on which side of the Atlantic one was when trying to manage paper currency. If not backed by something *real* and limited or scarce, prices were likely to spin out of control.

Despite the gloomy outcome, Edison could see hope in White's cautionary tale. The introduction of paper money (and subsequent issues) did at first lead to better economic conditions. Even White said that credit conditions eased and trade increased.[104] But, in a very few years, the system blew apart. Why?

---

[103] White, A.D., 1896, 1933, Introduction pages, dated September 1912.

[104] This is fully consistent with Hume's observation discussed above. Increasing gold and money leads at first to an increase in the output. This occurs because producers of goods (observing only a few prices — including that of their product) mistake rising prices in general that the increasing gold spurs, with a shift in demand towards their product in particular. This positive effect on trade reverses when full information works its way through the economy.

Edison could see why Hazlitt recommended White's book. It was obvious, though, that he had not explained himself very well in December. The ideas he sketched out on the banks of the Tennessee River were not about generating some fiat currency that had nothing real backing it. Edison knew from personal experience that purely fiat currency would not work. He was there when Civil War greenbacks inflated the price level. In his plan there would be something real as a basis for the currency.

Edison had hoped that the Federal Reserve Act, creating as it had, a number of 'banks for banks' in 1913, would deliver better economic performance than it had. But he also knew that the war was a huge dislocation that would have challenged a mature and long-standing central bank, let alone one that had to scramble to open doors by the end of 1914. Other than casting an interested eye on its progress through Congress, he had busied himself with technology. It took Ford in 1921 to jolt him out of his 'rut'.

Along with cautionary histories like White's, Edison also knew that many people had worked on the money problem through the years. Some of these had contributed to the discussions and debates surrounding the Federal Reserve Act.

If time had permitted, Edison could have dug deeper into the history of American money. It was full of frequent, loud, and urgent calls for changing the gold base of the system. His eyes would have lit up. Political 'money' movements coalesced to sometimes challenge, sometimes merge with one of the two major parties. Political fortunes rose and fell in part with the popular feeling of how well or poorly money was doing its job. The American monetary system always seemed to need either, just a bit of 'tweaking', or a complete overhaul depending on which 'camp' you were in.

It was complicated when one considered that the monetary system did not exist in a vacuum. National policies on taxes, tariffs, quotas, all involved creating winners and losers. Many interrelated groups were trying to influence national economic policies. Making sense of it all was daunting. The post-Civil War period of deflation was exacerbated by a rapid increase in transportation and farming capacity relative to the increase in population. Farmers, ranchers, growers, transportation and other services, small and large manufacturers, bankers, financiers, debtors, creditors, producers of tradable and non-tradable goods, importers, exporters, all had ideas on how national economic policies could be 'improved'. Making this even more complicated was the fact that these groups were not mutually exclusive.

Those in rural regions were taken very seriously and had tremendous political clout. In 1870, about three-fourths of the country's population was rural. Twenty years later, that percentage was lower, but still a large majority at 65% of the total. Farmers and their opinions mattered in legislatures from state capitols to Washington, D.C. Their opinion on gold-backed, referred to as 'hard' money, versus 'soft' or *fiat* money (money-by-law but with no metal backing at all) could differ depending on their circumstances. Those dependent on the export market and having little debt would be 'hard' money advocates. Farmers in debt and buying imported machinery, would lean towards 'soft' money. As a result, alliances formed and broke apart as circumstances changed. One 'scorecard' was never enough to keep track of all the players.

Trying to change the monetary system was just one of several economic levers that could be pushed or pulled in order for a group to attempt to achieve its goals. National economic policy included tariff policy and government expenditure and taxation policy.[105] Under pressure from one group or another, Congress changed tariffs no fewer than nine times between 1861 and 1913.[106]

In the same period the country went through nine changes in monetary and banking regimes, from the early 1830s *de facto* gold standard with no national banks up to the Civil War, inconvertible greenbacks (1862-1879), bimetallism — having two metals backing paper money — of one recipe or another (1879 to 1900), and then back to a single-metal, gold, standard (1900). Thrown into this mix, there were major changes in banking legislation, e.g. the National Banking Act of 1863, the Aldrich-Vreeland Act (1908), and the Federal Reserve Act of 1913.[107] At times monetary matters were central issues in presidential campaigns, at other times tariff policy predominated. The issues were economically interrelated, but political expediency and shifting interest group dynamics meant one or the other issue usually would be bubbling over.

A simple view of the monetary debate was that agrarian debtor-farmers aligned with newly influential 'free silver' western mining interests and pushed for soft-money policies that would unchain the dollar from gold. Minting silver would lead to a larger money supply

[105] A tariff is a tax on imported goods. If a tariff is imposed and the prices of imports rise accordingly, then domestic producers have less price competition from foreign sellers. A quota is a quantitative restriction on the number of units that may be imported — it has the same impact as a tariff as it serves to raise the price of imported goods.

[106] Congressional acts in 1861: Morrill, 1872, 1875, 1883: Mongrel, 1890: McKinley, 1894: Wilson-Gorman, 1897: Dingley, 1909: Payne-Aldrich, and 1913: Underwood. See Frieden (1996, 1997).

[107] This does not include numerous "free coinage" acts introduced, but failing to pass. The political process surrounding the creation of the Federal Reserve System also allowed many of these same battles to be replayed within the halls of Congress and in various committees in 1912 and 1913. These discussions featured both invited and uninvited input from academic economists, see Mehrling (2002), Dimand (2003).

and rising prices. The increased demand for silver would benefit the mining interests by raising the price for silver.[108] The rising prices of farm goods would reward the farmer with higher revenues. The rising price level would also lower the real value of farmers' debts.

Arrayed against this bloc supposedly were the northeastern creditor-bankers and financial interests who wanted the dollar tied to gold, to restrain inflation. Rather than leave the value of the currency up to politicians, this group wanted 'hard' money, where the gold value of the dollar is determined automatically through the discipline of the gold standard.[109]

In their opinion, a gold-standard, or 'hard', dollar would also make the U.S. a credible member of the world financial community. The dollar becoming an international currency was made more likely by eliminating the vagaries of exchange rate risk — stabilizing the international value of the dollar. Hoping to expand New York's role in the world's financial markets, New York City bankers, demanded a credible commitment to gold-backed dollars.

As Frieden (1996, 1997) has shown, the debtor-creditor view is too naïve. It does not explain Congressional voting patterns in the late 1800s-early 1900s. Not all farmers were debtors, not all debtors were farmers. An inflating currency is not a boon for all. A more nuanced view of the monetary situation from the mid-1800s onwards considers particular interests of smaller groups, e.g. farmers and manufacturers who trade internationally. Both of these groups may favor 'soft money' not for the real-debt lowering feature that inflation brings, but for the positive trade effects of the dollar's devaluation that inflation brings.

More deeply, manufacturers who might benefit from devaluation — more exports — would also benefit from protective tariffs (less foreign competition). They had to balance the political costs and benefits of trying to change monetary versus changing tariff policy. Farmers found gaining tariff protection for their crops difficult, though they had an interest in tariff policy because they bought machinery. Protective tariffs on imported manufactured goods would increase the prices of manufactured goods to farmers. The terms-of-trade turn against farmers if the prices they pay for manufactured goods rise faster than prices

---

[108] Silver interests were newly politically influential, especially proportionately more so in the Senate, as more western territories gained admission to the Union from the mid-1860s on.

[109] Following the Coinage Act of 1873, a victory for 'hard' money advocates which demonetized silver, the aggregate price level dropped by about 22% over the next six years. Thus the almost immediate agitation in the west and farm regions for allowing silver to rejoin the monetary system resulting in the silver-friendly Bland-Allison Act of 1878.

they receive for their crops. If their crops did not receive similar tariff protection, this was likely to be their fate.

Judging from the number of times policies changed these varying interest group collectives had success at different times. Tariffs on hundreds of goods went up and down, monetary changes swept across the country.[110] Groups had to compare costs and benefits of changing a particular national economic policy, e.g. tariffs, to the costs and benefits of changing another policy, e.g. the monetary system. If changing the monetary system to engineer an inflation-caused devaluation of the dollar is politically difficult, then these same farmers may join with others in fighting against an increase in tariffs on farm machinery imports and for lower tariffs in general.

Consider a very simple case splitting along two major fissures, debtor-creditor and importer-exporter, with the issue being: *Who is likely to support a policy that would cause inflation and a devaluation of the currency?*

		Are you a Debtor:	
		Yes	**No**
Are You an Exporter	**Yes**	Strongly Favor	Uncertain
	No	Uncertain	Strongly Oppose

Those who are in debt and rely on export earnings would strongly favor 'soft' money policies leading to inflation as it reduces the real value of the debt they owe and the devaluation of the dollar on world currency markets initially makes their exports easier to sell abroad. That's a 'win-win' for them.

Those on the other 'side' of both situations, lenders who do not rely on export earnings (or are even importers), would favor 'hard' money (no inflation) policies to maintain the value of the dollar in terms of gold and keep import (and import competing goods') prices from rising. Thus they would strongly oppose inflationary policies.

Mixed' cases, a debtor/importer for example, have uncertain outcomes and will depend on a case-by-case analysis of the benefits of the debt-reduction of inflation versus the harm of a devaluation raising

[110] For example, in 1909, the Payne-Aldrich Tariff Act, initiated to 'lower tariffs', raised tariff rates on 220 goods, lowered them on 650 goods, and left the rates on 1150 goods unchanged. Without a sophisticated (yet arbitrary) weighting scheme, it would be hard to claim that 'tariffs rose' or 'tariffs fell' as a result of this act, or any given tariff act.

import prices.[111] The larger ones' debt burden versus net import earnings the stronger one should favor a policy of inflation and devaluation and *vice versa.*

The Farmers Plan. Monetary plans abounded some with extremely strong interest-group and political support. Some plans fizzled with the political fortunes of their advocates. After the Civil War, the spread of the railroad and their freight rates, the Homestead Act, and the opening of mid-America stimulated many groups made up of the newly settled farmers.[112] These were social groups at first coalescing into political blocs. The blocs united farmers' interests and aggregated their dispersed power.

In the late 1880s south, the Southern Alliance, a farmer's group, proposed abolition of large banks, free coinage of silver, issuance of fiat paper money, and establishing sub-treasuries.[113]

The sub-treasury plan, pushed by one of their leaders, Charles Macune, addressed the *illiquidity* of farmers at crucial times in the crop cycle.[114] Traditionally, farmers experienced a shortage of money at harvest time when farmhands and other creditors, like the local bank, needed to be paid. With a great deal of their products hitting markets simultaneously, prices fell. Needing money (or *liquidity*), the farmer felt a victim of conspiring buyers and demanding lenders. Without a financial cushion, the farmer could not afford to withhold produce until prices rose. These were indeed the exact worries that that Edison heard from farmers.

To meet the farmers' needs, the sub-treasury in each county was to be supplied by the federal government with at least $500,000, and then would accept farmers' crops as collateral against which they could borrow 80% of their current local market value at an interest rate of 1%

---

[111] In the matrix, "Exporter No"=importer and "Debtor No"=lender. There is no third alternative. True, a more realistic picture might include those who are neither lenders nor debtors and neither importers nor exporters. On balance, members in this group should neither strongly favor nor oppose any given policy on inflation and devaluation. Thus, we omit them.

[112] These groups tried to bridge the loneliness of farm life and give them the power of a collective when dealing with large entities ranging from railroads, retail sellers of goods, governments, crop-buying brokers (and their financial backers). Mayhew (1972) argues that more than debt, or anger over low prices, which did not hit all farmers equally, nor necessarily describe their actual conditions, having to participate in the commercialization of their lives, losing their self-sufficiency — even if they were financially successful at the enterprise — made farmers particularly angry and this explains the farm-protest movement of the late 1800s.

[113] See Hicks, J.D., *The Populist revolt; a history of the Farmers' alliance and the People's Party*, [Lincoln] University of Nebraska Press, 1961 [c1959], chapter 7, pps. 186-204.

[114] While this idea is most associated with Macune (1851-1940) a leader of the Farmers Alliance, Hicks makes the case that Macune may have gotten the idea from a Harry Skinner (Hicks, *op cit.,* pg. 189).

per year.[115] If the crops were not redeemed within one year they could be sold to satisfy the debt. County governments would build and maintain the warehouses.

Farmers could sell the right to the stored crops for the difference between the current market price (the 'spot' price) and the 80% already paid out by the sub-treasury. The buyer, e.g. a miller, in the case of wheat, would then redeem the crops for the value of the loan, interest, storage and insurance costs. This would return the money to the sub-treasury.

As Macune saw it, the benefit of the plan was providing farmers money when they needed it without being pressured to sell on the lows of the over-supplied market. The money created would be 'retired' when the crops were withdrawn from the warehouse thus providing an 'elastic' — self-canceling — currency. It also took the banker out of the chain of transactions.

The plan had a brief, bright exposure, with hearings in Congress and supporting bills proposed, but it did not advance out of committees. By 1893 the idea had died even with its adherents in the Alliance. Most farmers threw their support behind the simpler, complementary and politically more potent message of free coinage of silver taken up by the charismatic William Jennings Bryan.[116]

Bryan and many planks of the Populist platform germinated in the prairie, agrarian, farm-based grange and alliance movements. He won three Democratic nominations to the presidency, but, despite his rhetorical skills, never the White House. The Democratic-Populist free silver coinage, bimetallic agenda, went no further.[117]

During the deliberations for the Federal Reserve Act, Bryan, by then Woodrow Wilson's Secretary of State, argued for a Federal Reserve District bank in every state; an echo, albeit faint, of the soft-money populist platform.[118]

'Hard' money interests prevailed led by Henry Parker Willis, serving as an expert to Carter Glass, Chair of the House Banking and Currency Committee responsible for drafting the House version of the

---

[115] Crops suggested were wheat, corn, oats, barley, rye, rice, tobacco, cotton, wool, and sugar. A handling, storage, and insurance charge was also proposed. As many as one thousand counties were suggested to participate.

[116] Macune also fell out with reformers over what they felt was duplicitous behavior in the election of 1892. He was forced to resign from the Alliance. Without its author, the plan had less chance of succeeding. With or without Macune, by 1893 the siren song of silver was loud enough to drown out the sub-treasury plan. See Hicks, op cit., page 204.

[117] Losing narrowly to hard money Republican William McKinley in 1896, losing by a wider margin in 1900, again to McKinley, and to William Howard Taft in 1908.

[118] Mehrling (1997, 2002) and Dimand (2003) provide extensive discussion on the economists, practical and academic, who either tried to or did have influence in the drafting of the Act.

Federal Reserve Act.[119] In order to provide 'elastic' currency, the Act allowed the Federal Reserve District banks — the banks for banks — to lend to commercial banks against short term loans made in support of industrial production. This is called the 'real bills' doctrine. Where a bank's bills (loans extended to businesses) for the production of 'real' output were used by these commercial (or 'retail') banks as collateral for loans they could receive from the Federal Reserve. These loans from the Federal Reserve were crafted to be self-canceling. As the real goods were sold in the market, firms and banks could pay off their loans. While 'elastic', the money supply would return to its long run steady state and the system should produce stable prices.[120] The Federal Reserve Act incorporated a gold-backed discipline on the issuance of paper money while allowing for some *elasticity* of money, especially at the regional level, as economic conditions dictated.

The Federal Reserve was designed to manage this elasticity by making fewer (tighter or less elastic) or more (easier, more elastic) loans to the retail banks as they needed. Regional business conditions — monitored by one of the twelve District banks — would partially drive Federal Reserve policy and over-all economic conditions — monitored by a Board in Washington, D.C. — would also be a factor. The Federal Reserve was implicitly expected to manage the nation's money so that an excess of it did not cause inflation. The reliance on gold as a backing was considered a long-run tether or anchor on the price level.

Irving Fisher of Yale University provided the strongest competition to the real bills doctrine at the time of crafting the Federal Reserve Act. His 'compensated dollar' plan called for backing dollars with gold, but allowed for a varying quantity of gold per dollar depending on the price level. The theory seemed sound, but most thought it impractical given its complexity, arbitrariness depending on price index used, and possibly harmful to U.S. trade.[121]

---

[119] Willis, who had had academic positions at Washington and Lee and George Washington Universities before taking the expert position with Glass's committee, was strongly influenced by his PhD chairman, J. Laurence Laughlin of the University of Chicago. Willis later taught at Columbia University, writing for various newspapers and journals, acted as an advisor to governments revising their monetary systems and served again as an expert for Carter's Senate committee drafting the Banking Act of 1933.

[120] Not everyone agreed that a 'real bills' system would be non-inflationary (e.g. see Humphrey, 1982), but this started anchored to gold and the international payments system at a fixed rate of exchange. The reason industrial loans were preferred is that the production process for mechanically produced goods is usually much shorter and subject to less disruption than agricultural production cycles.

[121] In an era of very little data collection beyond series on prices of individual goods, the concept of a single index number that could capture what was happening to many, potentially thousands of prices, was unfamiliar to most. Fisher was one of the few having done extensive work in the area. Who would manipulate the gold value of the dollar

Given the extensive debate and wrangling, President Wilson found himself 'surprised' to be signing the Act on December 23, 1913.

> "Wilson's amazement was justified in light of the many decades of bitter argument which had raged over many of the monetary issues the new system was attempting to solve."[122]

Eight short months later most of the world would be at war, most currencies unhinged from gold and the discipline of the gold standard abandoned. This had happened in war periods many times before with countries borrowing heavily to pay for their expenditures. World War One, being so widespread in nature, was a greater shock to national and international monetary systems than they had ever before experienced.

Four years later, nearing the end of the war, many economies lay in ruin. By mid-1921, the U.S. economy — victorious and never bombed — appeared to be one of those in deepest trouble. The inflation-deflation whipsaw was hitting everyone.

What went wrong? Could a really careful technician — America's Most Useful Citizen — design a better system? Was there a system that did not allow gold to straitjacket the dollar, but which had enough anchoring so that price pressures didn't blow it apart? Some anchor was necessary, Edison knew that from his readings of the *assignats* and his own post-war experiences, but the golden anchor gave too much power and control to one commodity.

Now that he'd bench-tested the current system and done his late-night reading, Edison, the innovator and inventor, plotted his attack.

(and when and how) was also a concern. The automaticity of the gold standard did not allow for such manipulation hence it provided an anchor assuring the dollar's value to international buyers of the dollar and dollar-denominated assets.
Through history many attempts and suggestions for stabilizing the purchasing power of money were produced, Irving Fisher's *Stable Money: A History of the Movement*, New York: Adelphi Company, 1934, is a good introduction.

[122] Dorfman (1949), page 340.

CHAPTER 7: NEW MONEY

"My reading during the last few months has covered a wide range of authorities and let me say that the midnight oil has not been spared. Having formulated in my mind some rudimentary ideas of what seemed to me a way out of many [problems]..."

"...I am supplementing my letter of yesterday...I have worked out a plan for helping the farmer in the future, and also one to make our currency stable.[123]

Engineering new, stable, money. For this to work Edison knew he had to keep the existing system intact. As much as he railed against it, gold-based money was too entrenched. People knew how it worked. The world's financial system, every bit as substantial as its communications network, was based on it. It had first-mover advantage. When he was developing quadruplex telegraphy, four messages at a time sharing one wire, Edison did not suggest ripping down all the existing telegraph poles. He did not suggest doing it without electric current. He knew he had to keep the existing parts. The financial system was no different:

"Any change whatsoever which affects 100 million people suddenly produces great losses until they have rearranged their affairs in line with the change."[124]

To prevent those massive losses, gold stays. So do the banks and the reviled 'money brokers, the money profiteers, the private bankers' charging interest "gain[ing] their power through a fictitious and false value given to gold." The commercial or retail banks — the ones on the corners of small town Main Streets — they stay, too. They did nothing wrong:

"Make it perfectly clear that I'm not advocating any changes in banks and banking. Banks are a mighty good thing. They are essential to the commerce of the country."[125]

Edison also learned the inflation lesson of the *assignats* and *greenbacks*. Paper money issued with no backing at all, despite all good intentions and the promises of the most upright and intelligent people, ultimately was over-issued leading to price inflations that spun out of control. Paper money, the money people were used to using, needed an anchor. However, the 'money profiteers' must not have excess power. One commodity — gold — should not be given too much value, ficti-

---

[123] Thomas Edison to J.S. Wannamaker, May 5 and 6, 1922

[124] Edison, "A Proposed Amendment to the Federal Reserve Banking System", Section R, May 13, 1922.

[125] *New York Times*, Dec. 6, 1921, page 6.

tious value at that, by being chosen by governments as *the* anchor. No *golden* sun would be at the center of his system.

So, where is Edison's problem? The problem is that Edison thought that gold brokers and dealers paid too little to the miner for gold, charged too much interest when they lent it to the Main Street bankers (who then passed this cost along to their borrowers), and kept too much profit for themselves. They were 'profiteers'. This caused the panics.

Despite the high hopes expressed on his sixty-seventh birthday back in February 1914, the nation's new central bank, The Federal Reserve, had not resolved the nation's financial problems. Here it was, 1922, more than seven years later and farmers were defaulting on their loans, losing their farms, and hundreds of banks were failing.

A constant refrain heard from farmers and the rural regions, now representing about half the nation's 106 million people, was that when money became scarce, they faced higher interest payments to borrow. They saw Wall Street squeezing banks in cities, city banks squeezing country banks, and then their country bank squeezing them right off their land. The instrument of pressure, torture almost, was the interest rate.

Edison excoriated those 'money profiteers' for setting this vicious extraction machine in motion, for charging interest on gold. Gold that was just *sitting idle* in their vaults! This is something the Devil would do, an 'invention of Satan'.[126] For Edison, a freethinker and religious skeptic, this view was not driven by religious fervor, but by his more practical belief that one should not pay for something that was merely idling, doing no apparent work.[127]

In this view, Edison had lots of big-name company. A substantial line of thought runs through time featuring thinkers like Aristotle, St. Thomas Aquinas, and Karl Marx all of whom believed charging interest on money was a sin. It even had a bad name: *usury,* and many states still have laws against charging interest rates that are 'too high' or 'usurious'.[128]

---

[126] Edison's friend, Henry Ford, would not sell cars on an installment — or interest — plan until 1924 spurred by competition with Chevrolet. Much of the Model T 'era' was primarily one of low-price, cash sales. Of course, in a very agrarian society, repossession costs might have been substantial.

[127] For Edison's views on religion, see Israel (1998), pps. 8-9, and 246-247.

[128] Current financial reform proposals are also suggesting that the federal government will be involved in determining interest rates to 'protect' consumers.

We will try to explain why we think Edison is wrong on this point. Wrong or right, he was in the company of some 'big' thinkers, he was not some lonely kook. Whether or not he would like to be seen sharing an idea with some of them, Karl Marx, for example, or — given his skepticism — Thomas Aquinas, well, that is an interesting conjecture. We do not have to assess whether or not Edison is right or wrong about interest,

Interest? Edison and others, like Aquinas and Marx, thought that was unreasonable. Why, remember, in the actual financial system of his day which he test-benched, the gold coins are just *sitting* in the vaults! They are not *doing* anything! Paper money and checking accounts are doing all the work. Why should someone get more money on idle money especially when it results in farmers losing their farms?

Back on the banks of the Tennessee River on that December morning, discussing Ford's financing scheme, Edison drove this point home repeatedly:

> "Now, that is what Henry Ford wants to prevent. He thinks it is stupid, and so do I, that for the loan of $30,000,000 of their own money the people of the U.S. should be compelled to pay $66,000,000 — that is what it amounts to with interest. People who will not turn a shovelful of dirt nor contribute a pound of material will collect more money from the United States than will the people who supply the material and do the work. That is the terrible thing about interest. In all our great bond issues the interest is always greater than the principal. All of the great public works cost more than twice the actual cost, on that account. Under the present system [bond finance] of doing business we simply add 120 to 150 per cent to the stated cost."

In Edison's opinion, Ford's financing plan is much better:

> "But, here is the point: if our nation can issue a dollar bond, it can issue a dollar bill. The element that makes the bond good makes the bill good, also. The difference between the bond and the bill is that the bond lets the money-brokers collect twice the amount of the bond and an additional 20 per cent., whereas the currency pays nobody but those who contribute to Muscle Shoals in some useful way."

How does Edison's math work out? How does $30 (we drop the extra zeros for simplicity) turn into $66? Edison's example requires time for repayment. Using his $30 figure, suppose that this principal is borrowed not for one year, but for twelve. Every year suppose that the lender charges simple interest of 10% of $30, or $3, as an interest payment. For eleven years that would add up to $3 x 11 = $33 in interest payments. The last, twelfth, year the final interest payment of $3 is paid and so is the principal sum of $30. So, at that point the bond matures and is totally repaid, $30 *plus* $36 interest! Borrow $30, pay back $66! How can the lender get away with that? Maybe bankers understood it, but to Edison it was high-finance trickery and protecting farmers from it was one of his goals.[129]

In early 1922, after his researches and test-benching, his way forward was clear to him:

---

we just need to know his views so that we understand why he wanted to relegate interest rates to a minor role or ultimately remove them altogether.

[129] Our example simplifies matters. Below we will go through Edison's example and show where we think he misses the essential element of interest payments.

(1) Paper money must be anchored. Even well-meaning and knowledgeable men mismanaged money into incredible inflations.

(2) Gold in the monetary system had to be retained otherwise the immense entrenched interests on Wall Street and in the Federal Reserve Banks would rise up in protest and kill his plan. Yet, gold's role in the monetary system needs to be reduced. More anchors are needed. Gold would be one of many anchors, not the *only* anchor.

(3) Edison would protect farmers from Wall Streeters. He would protect them from the interest rate terror. If the existing system had to stay, he would graft a parallel system on to the existing financial system that would remove the connection between farmers and Wall Street. He would leave the Federal Reserve and local banks untouched. If others had a financial plan and they liked it, they could keep it.

(4) To give farmers the flexibility of holding their crops, not having to sell upon harvesting into a market of plunging prices they would get warehouses. As they wrote to him in so many different voices: "...it remains a fact, as soon as the produce arrives at market in any great quantity, the price starts down...".[130] In his system, farmers would get interest-free loans without having to dump their crops on the market. They did not have to go to their local bank for a loan at interest unless they chose. If the local bank got squeezed by a big city bank getting squeezed by Wall Street, well, that pressure need no longer be applied to farmers. They would not get squeezed off their land.

He would devise a stable money system for farmers, interest-free, built on warehousing, preventing the price plunges to which indebted farmers were hostage. Ford had asked him to help the farmers and he thought he could. All of this without dismantling the incredibly complicated financial system already in place. As he viewed it, he offended no one and helped farmers. Writing:

> "Please note that my Plan changes nothing, — antagonizes no one. It does not change banking system, but just starts in a small way, goes on quietly and gets results.[131]

He had the outline of a plan in mind. Schematically the current system appeared like this to him: miners dug gold out of the ground, took their gold to the mint where the government minted it into coins at a rate of $20.67 per ounce. This price was set by the government.

Those coins entered the banking system and supported all the paper money and checking accounts that people used in transactions and borrowing and lending. Down at the bottom of the mining shaft, the miner was at the bottom of the monetary system. Now the money

---

[130] Vrooman to Edison, April 6, 1922. TENHP Banking 1922.

[131] Edison to Richard H. Edmonds, Editor, *Manufacturers Record*, Wenersville, PA, July 24, 1922. TENHP Banking 1922.

brokers and profiteers might end up controlling gold, but miners started with it.

What did this look like to miners? If it cost less than $20.67 per ounce to mine gold, gold mines ran day and night, miners were happy, and gold flowed to the mints. If it cost more than $20.67 to mine an ounce of gold and get it to the mint, gold mines closed. In this case, some people might melt down gold jewelry and bring it to the mint. Gold mine owners and their representatives in Congress would probably call for a revaluing of gold and dollars. So, even the *golden* anchor had some slippage.

Meanwhile, farmers usually had to take out a loan in the spring, to be repaid — if all went well — by the harvest in the fall. They did not know in the spring what the price would be in the future. If prices were as high (or higher) than farmers were hoping when they planted, then all would be well (assuming they had a crop). If prices fell or crops were ruined by droughts, hail, floods, farmers defaulted on their loans and were driven from their land. If money got tight and interest rates rose, then farmers defaulted. Three things could happen to farmers and two were bad.

Yet, gold from the ground, corn (or wheat, or cotton, or sugar) from the ground, why should they be treated differently? So, Edison, perhaps borrowing from the sub-treasury plan of the late 1800s, suggested government warehouses where farmers could bring their crops. At that point, the government would give them a set amount of paper money for their crops. The amount they would receive would be set by the average price of that crop over the past twenty-five years. So, if a crop's price had been rising through time, Edison's fixed payment would reflect that, but with a lag. Farmers would retain ownership rights to their crops, which they could sell at any time; if they — or to whomever they sold their crops — wished to get the crops out of the warehouse they had to repay the money given to them.

The government warehouses did three things: they turned crops into money at a known rate, as the government mint did with gold; they allowed the farmer storage so that crops did not have to be sold into a falling market, no "jam up of markets"; and they created multiple anchors for money. He even drew a little sketch (shown on the following page) so the reader could *see* what he meant:[132]

[132] Edison to Wannamaker, May 12, 1922. TENHP Banking 1922.

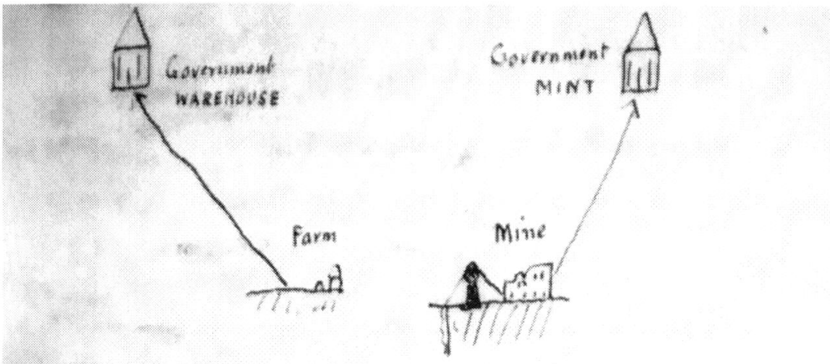

Gold miner brings his commodity to the Mint. It is graded, and he receives its full value in gold certificates and pays no interest. Costs Government nothing except expense of printing the paper certificate. The Government does not charge the miner anything for grading because it is so anxious to get this commodity that it foregoes this charge.

To cast out the 'interest' Devil, Edison suggested that the money given the farmer should be at zero interest. Whenever farmers chose, they could redeem their crops from the warehouse for the money 'lent' them and then sell the crops. Farmers could also sell their right to the stored crops to others, if they so wished. These buyers would have to pay the warehouse the amount of money given to the farmers to gain the crops. The important point being, farmers had time to figure out what they wanted to do and when they wanted to do it with their crops. They could sell them immediately upon harvesting, if they liked the current market price. They could store them in hopes of a higher price later; or, they could sell their right to their crop in the warehouse at any time. Any of these three ways, they were going to get money immediately.[133] In Edison's plan, three things could happen to farmers and they were all good.

Farmers would deal with the government-operated warehouses and commodities markets. All loans would be interest-free. The warehouses might make a small charge to cover their costs of storage, but they would have no incentive to take advantage of farmers.[134] Now the farmer, almost any farmer, was like the gold miner. These crops were new, additional anchors, for the paper money supply.

What about money? Edison thought that was the prettiest point. The warehouses would be giving out paper money from the Federal Reserve banks, backed by the crops entering the warehouse,

[133] We go through the details and mechanics of Edison's plan below.

[134] In response to his inquiries, Edison received several letters detailing ways that farmers were 'cheated' by mis-grading, mis-weighting, and under-payment by privately operated elevators and warehouses.

when it was needed. Then when the farmers (or whoever owned the right to the crops) returned and removed their crops they would repay the money:

> "There is no credit or promises introduced. The currency varies in exact proportion as it is needed and it contracts exactly as the commodities move. Removing these violent changes in demand for currency on account of the season the commercial bank is relieved of these strains and disturbances."[135]

At this point, Edison wanted to make sure that he had not stumbled somewhere. In his electrical work, he had developed a careful research protocol. He usually put together research teams to work out all the aspects of an invention.[136] Sometimes what seemed like a good idea did not translate into a marketable product. It was always better to find this out sooner rather than later. Nor was there any shame in being wrong, "I have not failed. I've just found 10,000 ways that won't work."[137]

This work on money he could not give to the boys in the machine shop or battery labs. Even if he were still there, that sarcastic, theory-oriented, Nikola Tesla — "Our Parisian"[138] — would be of little use in the financial realm. While he had many experts in electrical *current*, in January of 1922 Edison needed experts in *currency*.

He had the outline of a plan, and he wanted nothing more than to be put right if he was wrong. But, he did not want the experts — if they could be identified — to read through a lengthy plan and then pass a single verdict, "*Yea*" or "*Nay*". No, that would tell him little. His plan had interrelated elements, many 'moving parts', multiple anchors, warehouses, interest-free loans. He needed to know which was weak, if it was, and which were strong. In this way, weaknesses could be addressed and the invention improved where needed. That's how he and the teams always did it, piece by piece, part-by-part. How many filaments had they tested?

Rather than sending off a complete plan, or blueprint, from A to Z, in January of 1922 he devised a set of twenty-six questions; each making the expert think carefully about each of the plan's elements, its structure, and then comment question-by-question. He thought he had the solution to the nation's money woes, but now it was time to find out what the experts thought.

In early February Edison readied the questions, the addresses, the envelopes and then sent his assistant off to the post office with the hefty carton of outgoing mail.

---

[135] Edison, "A Proposed Amendment...", May 13, 1922, section S.

[136] Israel (1998), chapter ten.

[137] This and similar sentiments attributed to Edison.

[138] Baldwin (1995), pps. 200-202.

CHAPTER 8: THE QUESTIONNAIRE AND THE EXPERTS

"...I prepared a questionnaire containing twenty-six questions and sent it around to a number of Bankers and Economists in various parts of the country."[139]

Twenty-six questions on their way to the experts. What did Edison want to know? We have an idea of his system, schematic diagram and all. We'll look at the questions and see how they fit in with 'testing' his proposal. Other than knowing that these had to be written between the visit to Muscle Shoals in early December 1921 and their sending to the experts in late January and early February 1922, we have no further idea of how or exactly when Edison created them.

There is some obvious repetition and some seem totally divorced from his plan. We'll try to decipher them and tie them together. Unfortunately, that isn't always easy without help from Edison explaining exactly why he thought a question important. This help is non-existent. Thus, in places a best-guess is required.[140]

(1) What, in your opinion, would be the approximate market value of a Troy ounce of pure gold if all the Governments of the World should demonetize it?

Edison, as we saw above, knows that a new proposal can not hope to be successful if it dislocates the finances of over 100 million people. His system does not 'demonetize' gold, that is, remove it as an anchor or backing, as much as he would like to do this. However, by introducing more anchors his plan de-emphasizes gold. He would like to know what gold would be worth if there were no demand for it as a monetary anchor.[141] This would give a lower bound on its value.

Gold's value at the time was $20.67 per ounce.[142] Remove the monetary demand for it and one expects that to drop. How far? Very far and holders of gold would not be pleased. But, if the experts thought that its value would fall little then gold holders would suffer only small losses. Their opposition to his plan might then be muted. On the other hand, if the estimated drop was large Edison could expect dramatic opposition to his plan.[143]

---

[139] Edison to Wannamaker, May 5, 1922, Banking 1922, TENHP.

[140] For someone willing to try 10,000 ways, maybe we should be happy that he stopped at twenty-six questions. The questionnaires are in Banking 1922, TENHP.

[141] Of course, there would still be a demand for it as a useful metal.

[142] About $275 in today's (2011) dollars.

[143] If the price of gold falls too far, gold holders might even wish to send it abroad where it might have higher value. Edison thought gold holders were generally sophisti-

(2) If the U.S. Government were to build fireproof concrete sectional warehouses at desirable points, using therefore money received from taxation, and should receive, grade and store, for *stated periods of time,* (say, one year) selected necessities of life: Issue a certificate or receipt for same, and should enact a law that the U.S. District Treasury, or the Federal Reserve Bank, might issue 50% of the market value of these commodities in money, (such market value being based on the average selling price over a period of 25 years and so endorsed on the certificate), would this money, so issued, be sound money? If not sound money, give your reason.

Here are some specifics of the plan's detail. Crops may be stored for up to one year; the farmer receives 50 percent of their value in Federal Reserve bank notes (paper money), this value determined by their average market prices over the past twenty-five years.

Is that paper money "sound money"? This is the heart of Edison's plan, getting money to farmers. As he writes to many people, this is the most important question of them all.[144] If it is "sound money", sound as any other paper money (from which it is indistinguishable) then in use, his plan is credible. If it is not sound, then the experts will tell him why not and he can fix it.

(3) Would the money thus issued be as sound as a dollar secured by, say, 50 cents worth of gold, and the promise of the Government? I mean in the ultimate analysis and not considering the gambling chance that it is very unlikely that everyone would want their gold at once.

Just in case the experts are not paying attention, Edison re-asks the question a slightly different way. Gold-backed paper money; would the new money be as sound as gold backed money? If so, then it is "sound"; if not, his experts will tell him and he'll fix it.

(4) If the answer to No. 2 is that the money issued on a U.S. Government Warehouse certificate and held as security, is sound money, (the equity in which is owned by the owner of the certificate and upon which he has received 50% of the market value) would this equity be available of being discounted by a commercial bank? Would the currency thus received from the Federal Reserve Bank be sound money: the capital and surplus of the bank being in money issued in the first instance?

In plain words: as in question 2, the farmer gets paper money immediately. Along with that, he receives an equity (ownership) certificate representing her ownership in the deposited crop. One needs that certificate and the money the warehouse paid out to reclaim the crop. Is that certificate likely to be accepted as collateral at the farmer's bank,

---

cated and did not need him as an advocate. However, how sophisticated were gold miners? Edison did not seem worried about them. Maybe they could become farmers.

[144] For example, he writes a note to his assistant on a letter from a E.S. Brownson, Sr., from Brooklyn, NY: "Tell him to answer number 2 of Questions as that's the pith of the whole thing." March 23, 1922, Banking 1922, TENHP.

a Main Street bank? If so, then the farmer has a really good deal. He gets cash from the warehouse and he can get a loan based on her ownership share of the crop, if he wishes.

(5) If this second issue of money is unsound money, point out why it is more unsound than the present money, based on gold and silver and promises?

If the money lent by the banks is unsound, why? This extends the backing questions (#2 and #3 above) to the paper money that banks might lend using the warehouse equity certificates as collateral. If it is deemed sound, then his plan is that much sounder.

(6) If money is issued on selected necessities of life (held and in control of the Government) to the extent of 50% of their value, could there thus be any inflation of the currency due to this particular issue? Would farmers over-produce so as to stock up these warehouses to get a loan of 50% of the value of their produce and thus inflate or multiply the currency?

A currency that caused inflation would be unsound, so the first question appears to be questions #2 and #3 again. The second part, would farmers 'over'-produce, is very interesting. It recognizes that behavior changes when incentives change. Edison is asking for 'dynamic' scoring of his plan, not 'static' scoring. That is, he wants the experts to forecast if farmers would have an incentive to produce more than they normally would in anticipation of selling the government the crops.[145]

(7) Suppose that through these Government warehouses the issue of money should far exceed, per capita, the highest amount that so far has been issued and more than is necessary to transact business, would there arise any danger similar to what has occurred with currency not backed by reasonable amount of gold?

Do we have to worry about the *assignats/greenbacks* inflationary experience? If we do, then the system is unsound.

(8) If England had government warehouses wherein were certain selected articles from her Colonies which articles America buys and will probably always buy, and such articles are inspected by and guaranteed by the English Government which should issue a special currency on the warehouse certificate at one-half the market value of the goods, would this special currency facilitate the exchange of commodities more than now with present difference in money?

---

[145] If the plan is good for the farmer, then it may lead to an increase in land prices because it would be good to be a farmer. That benefits current farm land owners who are not always farmers. It would be expected to raise the rent of farm land. Edison might also have asked if crops would flow to the U.S. from Canada and Mexico, crossing the border in search of U.S. money? There might be many responses by many affected individuals to a new program like Edison's.

This appears to be a question aimed at whether or not a plan like his can facilitate (or at least leave unharmed) international trade and exchange. It is a little at odds with his plan, though, as he indicates a 'special currency' would be produced by England. Yet, he has been very careful in his plan as it applies in the U.S., to highlight that the paper money paid out to farmers from the warehouses would be identical to all other Federal Reserve notes (paper money). In the U.S., no special currency is being created.

(9) Would not this special currency, issued in the manner stated, by any stable government in which we have confidence, purchase more goods in the USA than their normal currency, based on a small quantity of gold and credit?

Edison's intent becomes clearer. Is this 'special currency' preferred, unit for unit, to the normal currency because it has (or may have) more goods backing it? We'll see what the experts say. Obviously, if they prefer the 'special currency' he has a vote for that part of his plan as all he has to do is change the word "England" and phrase "stable government in which we have confidence" to "the U.S." and he's back to his plan.

(10) Assuming that the US Government still owned many square miles of territory which, if irrigated, would be worth many times as much money per acre than land subject to the vicissitudes of climate, and should build a dam and reservoir for power and irrigation, leasing the land on rental and contracting out the power, and should issue currency to build the dam and ditches and construct the power station, would this currency be sound money? It is backed by actual value which continues for ever. Would it not have a value as great as the 100 million of 1st Mortgage Bonds of the Union Pacific Railroad, the property of which is far less permanent bringing a lower income, leaving out of consideration the danger which all such projects contain of being abused by legislative action in times of financial peril?

In his plan, Edison did not mention electricity. In fact, he emphasized warehouses, interest-free loans for farmers, and self-canceling money. Except for the day along the Tennessee River and Ford's particular scheme—one which Edison did not build in to his plan — this question seems out of place, extending, as it does, the commodity backing of Edison's plan to the backing of currency with possible electricity sales. One guess is that he put this in as a favor to Ford to get a feel for what experts thought of Ford's scheme.

Given we have no idea of how much power he thinks can be generated, the price at which it can be sold, and the length of time that may run, trying to compare that fuzzy stream of expected value with railroad bonds of some known marketable value, is virtually impossible.

His last codicil is crucially important to many elements of the plan: "...leaving out of consideration the danger which all such projects contain of being abused by legislative action in times of financial peril?"

(11) If you answer that it is not sound money, is it for reason for its lack of ready convertibility, like the currency issued for goods in the warehouses which may be sold at once? Why is this lack of convertibility serious? Explain what bad effects would occur in case of a depression or panic, when, say 90% of our currency was issued for one-half of the value of necessities of life and 10% issued on projects like this land and irrigation operation, not separately, but both back of a uniform currency of one character and made unchangeable by amendment to the Constitution by popular vote, so that this ratio of 90% and 10% could not be changed.

Again, his intent becomes a bit clearer. If one claims that a "pure" Ford scheme is unsound, could one weld Edison's 'sound' (he's anticipating that verdict) money with Ford's less sound one to form sound money? Might not a bi-backed scheme like this provide needed purchasing power in time of depression? Is 'wobbly' money better than none?

(12) On the other hand, suppose the Government operated the dam and sold the land, charging rental for water, would this enhance the value of the currency issued to put the scheme in operation? The currency would be redeemed in this case rather quickly. Would this make this currency more sound and desirable?

'Okay, if you do not like Ford's scheme, how about in addition we back the electricity backing the currency with water, too?' Now does Ford's scheme look sounder? It will be interesting to see what the experts make of this.

(13) Do you think that civilized countries have, from experience and knowledge of economics, reached a stage where they could drop the fiction, unreality and chaotic state of a currency based on gold, and adopt a money, back of which is real useful wealth of twice the value of the money issued? Must we always remain on a gold basis? Is it beyond the wit of man to devise any equivalent method?

Edison seems to be asking if his plan is not better than the current gold standard. The reader cannot help but notice that his language is loaded against the gold standard.

(14) If all civilized countries have not reached that point, then state what countries, in your opinion, have advanced to that point.

Which countries have managed to throw off their chains of gold?

(15) Could gold be demonetized in the U.S. at some future time, except for paying international balances, and a national currency established, based on real wealth, as stated, without any great disturbance?

Could I, Thomas Edison, possibly be right?

(16) Suppose such a currency was issued, as I have described, would this increase or diminish the profits of our banking system? Take into consideration the possibility of a great increase of wealth, possible from a 100% sound currency and its ready availability.

Wealthier people probably use banks, and more intensively, than poorer people. So, if we assume that wealth rises, might not banks share in that increased wealth? Is he assuming the answer he wishes the experts to give him?

(17) When a bank discounts the note of a merchant and charges 7% (which is called interest) isn't this a misnomer? Does not the bank perform certain duties and services for this 7% that is worth it? Why call it interest? Why don't they enlighten the public? A person loaning money to a railway, taking bonds, gets interest but he performs no service like a bank. Yet both are called "interest."

A bank lends money to a merchant holding his note, or I Owe You (I.O.U.) as collateral. If the merchant defaults, the banker has the note and the legal right to attempt to get repaid. The note may actually have something solid backing it, the merchant's wares, or house, etc. The bank performs the service of providing purchasing power to the merchant which the merchant uses as he sees fit — he may pay for resources, including labor, to make more products.

A person lending money to a railroad holds the railroad's bonds (IOUs) as collateral. The person lending the railroad money performs the same service as the bank above — he lends the railroad purchasing power which it may use to buy rails, or rolling stock, or whatever, and sell more product, freight or passenger tickets. The railroad's IOU may be backed by collateral.

Edison seems to be making a distinction where there is none. Payments for services seem admissible to him, interest payments seem inadmissible—we already know they're 'the invention of Satan.' Are the services of money 'the invention of Satan'?

(18) If by some financial system brought into being and made the law by legislative action, whereby the money issued cannot be 100% sound, and this money is loaned to a railroad, taking bonds payable, principal and interest, in gold, is there not a chance that in this exchange the lender is getting more interest and more surety of his principal than he is entitled to?

If you buy something worth $10 for $5, aren't you coming out ahead unfairly?[146]

(19) Before the war German currency was on a gold basis; today he has many millions of gold in the Reichsbank. Isn't he still on a gold basis? If not, at what particular state of her holdings of gold did he cease to be on a gold basis?

At the time Edison wrote this, late January 1922, the German

[146] Under these circumstances we would expect to see railroad bonds priced differently in gold as opposed to that less-than 100% sound money.

mark had fallen almost 99% in value against the U.S. dollar compared to its pre-war value. Ironically, it had yet to enter its soon-to-be infamously notorious hyperinflationary phase. That was coming in 1923.

It is hard to see where Edison wants to go with this question. If the experts say that Germany *is* on a 'gold basis', then Edison may retort that it is pretty variable in value.[147] On the other hand, if the experts say that Germany is not on a 'gold basis', then the question does not really yield any new information. Edison already knew that unbacked money could be over-issued with inflation resulting.

(20) Do you believe that governments should base their money on gold after we have seen that on account of special disturbances, such as one country taking most of the gold to itself, disturbing the commerce of the world, and bring about a state of affairs that they can't trade with each other; do you think it beyond the power of man to improve on his crude mechanizm (sic) of commerce?

Could any other monetary standard have survived the vicissitudes of a world war better than did the gold standard?

(21) Do the words "fiat money" mean that money, not redeemable in gold at par, is fiat money?

Fiat means law. Fiat money is therefore "money by law". The experts might wonder what Edison is getting at with this question. It appears to be a tautology.

(22) If this is correct, no country has enough or ever had enough gold to redeem all its money in gold, at par. How much of the whole body of money is good money and how much fiat money?

So, if fiat money is fiat money, there is not enough gold to redeem it "at par."[148] Take Edison's premise, let "par" be $10 per ounce of gold. If there are 10 ounces of gold in the vault and there are $100 in paper notes, then all money is "good money" because, by definition, it can be redeemed at par. If there are more than $100 in paper notes (say $200), money trades below par, $20 per ounce. Is half the money "good" and half "fiat"? If so, if all the money looks the same, which half is which?

(23) Gold can be made a standard, but it is not possible to make any known piece of matter a standard of value. Nothing is known that will not vary in value to man or men. Is there any truth in this statement?

---

[147] By 'gold basis' we can only guess that Edison means paper money redeemable at some fixed rate for gold.

[148] One wonders who sets "par". If I get to set it, I can set a "par value" to make sure that there is enough gold to redeem even the greatest number of paper notes that one can print.

Let the experts speak. They are probably inclined to agree to the second two statements.

(24) If so, what value is gold as a standard if the currency issued against it is in excess of the gold whose value is constantly varying?

If gold cannot provide an unvarying, unyielding, absolute standard of value, why use it as a money standard?

(25) The subject matter of Andrew D. White's work called *Fiat Money Inflation in France* is used as a terrible example. Is it not true that there are two sides to this question, of which White gives only one side? France, just before the issue of assignats, was hopelessly bankrupt and would have been worse off without assignats than with them. There were great compensations for the depreciation of assignats, which ultimately caused France to become one of the richest nations. The fiat money of our Revolution became worthless directly and 1000% good indirectly. This is no argument for fiat money, as, in my opinion, all general money within a country should have practically twice the value of its par behind it.

During the period when people under-predicted the rate of inflation, real economic activity increased. Just as when, on the test bench, we increased the number of gold coins and people had more to spend on all goods, prices rose and producers made more goods. Unemployment fell. Weren't those good times worth the pain and losses of the bust that followed when inflation overtook economies?

Or, if they had not had "the fiat money of our Revolution" ('Continentals'), perhaps the war would have been lost. So, those holders of worthless Continentals financed a winning war effort which was better for them than losing to the British. Or, perhaps winning a war 'poor' is better than losing 'wealthy'. In effect, the Continental holders paid the taxes that won the war. A punishing inflation was just a way of taxing the people that was easier to administer than a "real" tax, like an income tax. But, as those holders of Continentals found out, inflation is a tax, a very real tax.

(26) Germany has issued and is now issuing enormous quantities of fiat money. This appears to be serious. Yet all her people are working furiously. America, it is said, has no fiat money. Four million men are idle, living off the workers and we have depression in business. The same case in England. Point out why this is so and what will probably be the final result.

Let the experts speak. One point is obvious, when people are facing rapidly rising prices, prices rising faster than their incomes, they feel and are worse off. When they are worse off they have to work harder and longer to try to stop falling back further and get back to where they were. There were also different institutional factors, like tax liabilities, at play among the countries named.

As these questions make obvious, Edison worked intensely between December 5, 1921, and the end of January 1922, learning as much as he could about money, banking, and systems, current and ancient. He formed a plan — aspects of which we have seen — and then he asked very specific questions of his experts in order that they might set him right if he went wrong. Edison did not give them his plan in its entirety. Given the publicity surrounding his and Ford's trip to Muscle Shoals, and given a couple of the questions, some experts could probably intuit the purpose of his questions. Others, perhaps unfamiliar with Ford's scheme and Edison's traipsing along the banks of the Tennessee River, must have looked at the questionnaire and wondered where it had come from and what was its purpose?

One thing they knew for sure. It came from Orange, New Jersey, and the polite cover letters asking their help were signed by Thomas A. Edison. The experts took notice. Now it is our turn to notice them. Who were the handpicked research team that Edison put on to this project and what did they recommend? Was this invention flawless — would it burn bright and long? Or, were there problems in the 'machinery'. Edison wanted to know: "My object in asking the questions [is] simply to obtain information and explanations from the experts, i.e., the economists and bankers."[149]

[149] Edison to Editor, *Topeka Capital*, Topeka, KS, April 12, 1922. Banking 1922, TENHP.

CHAPTER 9: THE EXPERTS SPEAK

"So far, bankers and economists who have answered do not seem to have understood the questions at all. They jump right in, and, without reading carefully, say that I argue for fiat money and throw French Assignats, Continental Money and Greenbacks at me."[150]

Twenty-six questions on their way to seventeen men, Edison's hand-picked stable-money research team. Ten are academic or Federal Reserve economists and seven from the business-banking community.[151] The Federal Reserve members and economists are:

J. H. Case, Deputy Governor of the New York Federal Reserve Bank (New York Fed),
W.P.G. Harding, Governor of the Federal Reserve Board in Washington, D.C. (the 'Ben Bernanke' of his day),[152]
Pierre Jay, Chairman of the New York Fed,
E.W. Kemmerer, Professor of Economics and Finance, Princeton University;
A.C. Miller, Board member, Federal Reserve System, Washington, D.C.,
E.M. Patterson, Professor of Economics, University of Pennsylvania,
William A. Scott, Professor of Economics, University of Wisconsin,
O.M.W. Sprague, Professor of Banking and Finance, Harvard University,
N.A. Weston, Professor, University of Illinois,
H. Parker Willis, Professor of Banking, Columbia University.

The seven businessmen-bankers were:

C.H. Crennan, economist at the Continental & Commercial National Bank of Chicago,
J.B. Forgan, Chairman of the Board, First National Bank of Chicago,
Arthur Reynolds, Continental & Commercial National Bank of Chicago,
Paul M. Warburg, Chairman, International Acceptance Bank, New York,
H.A. Wheeler, VP Union Trust Company of Chicago,

---

[150] Edison to Hugh W. Sanford, Knoxville, TN, March 8, 1922, Banking 1922, TENHP.
[151] "List of names to whom Money Questionnaires have been sent," undated, Banking 1922, TENHP.
[152] Despite the similarities, this Harding, originally from Alabama, is not the U.S. president nor is he related.

C.E. Mitchell, President, National City Bank of New York,
Darwin P. Kingsley, New York Life Insurance.

It is unclear where Edison got these names or how he decided who would be on the list of all-stars. Many of these likely were 'household names' of the day. Several of the academics were well-known internationally as well as nationally. Kemmerer, Sprague and Willis had high profiles as they consulted with governments and they were widely quoted in the press. Kemmerer was known as "the international monetary doctor" and was on a job in Brazil when Edison's questionnaire caught up with him. Sprague, no stranger to government service as well as academe, had a long career and a significant role in the Monetary Commission of 1908-1912 that was the precursor of the founding of the Federal Reserve System. In 1933, he was a special assistant to the U.S. Treasury Secretary when he resigned his post protesting F.D. Roosevelt's monetary (gold) policy.

Henry Parker Willis was well known in the New York financial press and in Washington, D.C., for his work on the Federal Reserve Act. He earlier consulted in Europe on the Latin Currency Union, Ireland's central bank, and in Asia with the Bank of the Philippines. A.C. Miller was a former professor at the University of California, now a member of the Federal Reserve Board. Yale's Irving Fisher arguably was better known for his knowledge of money — and his work on stable money — than any of these, yet he was not on the original list.[153]

Among the businessmen-bankers, Paul Warburg, "the intellectual father of the Federal Reserve" was one of the best known and respected bankers on both sides of the Atlantic; Charles "Sunshine Charlie" Mitchell headed the largest bank in the country.[154]

Almost immediately returns stream in to Orange. As shown on the following page, Warburg and Weston decline politely:[155]

[153] Perhaps Edison thought he would not be objective given he was actively pushing his own monetary plan.

[154] Both appellations from Ahamed (2009), page 312. Warburg and Mitchell, relatively speaking, were the Brian Moynihan (Bank of America), Jamie Dimon (JP Morgan-Chase), or Vikram Pandit's (Citibank) of their day. During the later stock market crash of 1929, Mitchell, who had made the National City Bank into one of the nation's largest banks via aggressive stock market activity, was blamed by no less than Senator Carter Glass for the market's gyrations and collapse. Mitchell was forced to resign from National City bank in 1933, indicted, tried for tax evasion, acquitted in 1934. He later rebuilt his fortune and reputation on Wall Street. See Wikipedia: http://en.wikipedia.org/wiki/Charles_E._Mitchell.

[155] Banking 1922. TENHP.

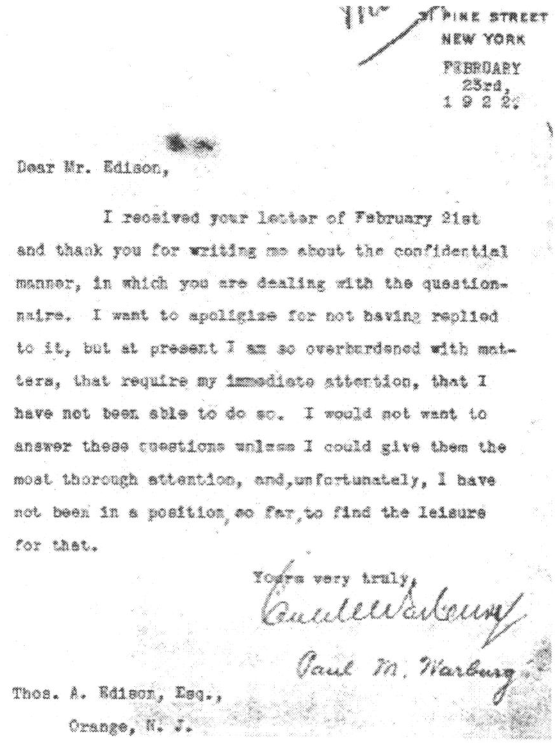

17 Pine Street
New York
February 23rd, 1922.

Dear Mr. Edison,

I received your letter of February 21st and thank you for writing me about the confidential manner, in which you are dealing with the questionnaire. I want to apoligize for not having replied to it, but at present I am so overburdened with matters, that require my immediate attention, that I have not been able to do so. I would not want to answer these questions unless I could give them the most thorough attention, and, unfortunately, I have not been in a position so far, to find the leisure for that.

Yours very truly,
Paul M. Warburg
Paul M. Warburg.

Thos. A. Edison, Esq.,
Orange, N. J.

Weston's letter, while polite, has a little more 'bite', indicating his impatience with the confusing nature of the wide-ranging questions. Upon his reading, Edison directs his assistant to respond encouraging Weston to focus on Question No. 2 —"the important one":

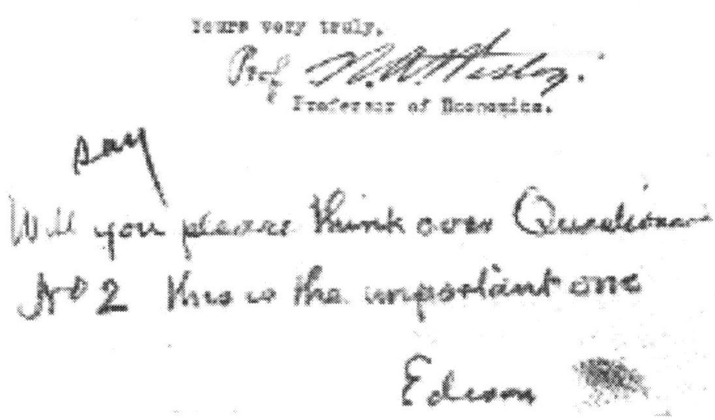

Yours very truly,
Prof. [signature]
Professor of Economics.

Say
Will you please think over Question No 2 this is the important one
Edison

Between February 6 and April 3, eight sets of answers, some very detailed, come in from Harding, Patterson, Forgan, Mitchell, Kingsley, Crennan, Kemmerer, and Jay.[156]

Also coming in are letters from people from around the country. What's this? The questionnaire has gotten out — gone viral! — stirring up great interest. This does not happen to inventors and their research teams when they are working on inventions in their labs, behind locked doors. The work is top-secret. But, it was happening to Edison.

On February 21, a Minneapolis paper writes him asking for a copy of the questions citing a newswire report. Edison directs his assistant to: "Say it was not intended to publish the Questions but the *NY World* got hold of a copy somehow and published it — E"[157]

Edison acts to mollify his research team who may not wish their answers to go public. Writing to Federal Reserve Board Governor Harding, February 21, 1922, he explains:[158]

> "Allow me to say, for your information, the Questionnaires are kept under lock and key in my office and I have no idea of how the newspapers obtained a copy. It was obtained from some source unknown to me, and published without my knowledge or consent."

Once out, the genie can not be put back in the bottle. The country now knows that Thomas Edison — the great inventor — is working on the monetary system and he's asking for advice. Some or all of the questions are in the press. Within the next month seventeen more copies of the questionnaire are in the mail headed to the curious from England to California, Alberta to Texas.

This unintended release also stimulates interesting exchanges between Edison and noted financiers and economists who did not make the 'first cut' as well as with the farmers he is trying to help.[159] Irving Fisher, Roger Babson, Bernard Baruch, and Arthur Kitson in England, among others engage with him in an exploration of his questions and his monetary theory. He hopes that their ideas improve his thinking.[160]

Edison also uses this added publicity to set up meetings with the *New York Times* and its financial reporter Garet Garrett. Later in

---

[156] There is no record of any response from Case, Miller, Reynolds, Sprague, or Wheeler.

[157] *The National Leader*, to Edison February 21, 1922. Banking 1922. TENHP.

[158] Edison to Harding, February 21, 1922. Banking 1922. TENHP.

[159] Material from many of those letters was used in earlier chapters.

[160] Because these are well-known men of their day for finance and economics and because their reasonably extensive correspondence with Edison reflects their views on the questions I add them to the "research team".

July 1922 the *Times* will have a large feature on Edison and his monetary proposal.

Edison needs to read the answers, tweak his model, and then have the technical details, the "blue print" of his proposal, ready to go. The questions may have gotten out, but it appears that the answers — at his end — are still secure. Edison tries to put that distraction behind him and then the Scott Affair hits.

Lacking a response, Edison's method is to follow up on the questionnaire within a few weeks. For example, having written to Henry Parker Willis on February 3 and perhaps missing Willis's very testy refusal of February 6, Edison 'tickled' him later in the month. Willis's response —

> "Your letter of February 21 is at hand…However, I wrote you some days ago [Feb. 6] that I did not believe in this method of approaching a scientific subject, and being unable to adapt myself to it, I begged to be excused from further commenting on the questions."

— obviously raises Edison's ire as he scribbles across the top of the letter:

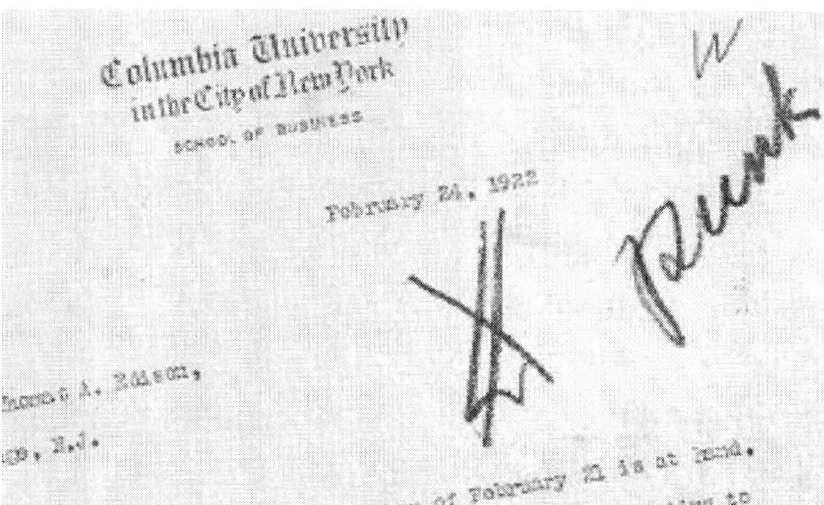
Columbia University in the City of New York

SCHOOL OF BUSINESS

February 24, 1922

W

Bunk

[161]

If Willis is brusque and has the audacity to tell him what is and is not 'science', then his colleague William Scott of Wisconsin is downright insulting:

[161] Willis to Edison. February 24, 1922. Banking 1922. TENHP. Reproduced in Hammes and Wills (2004).

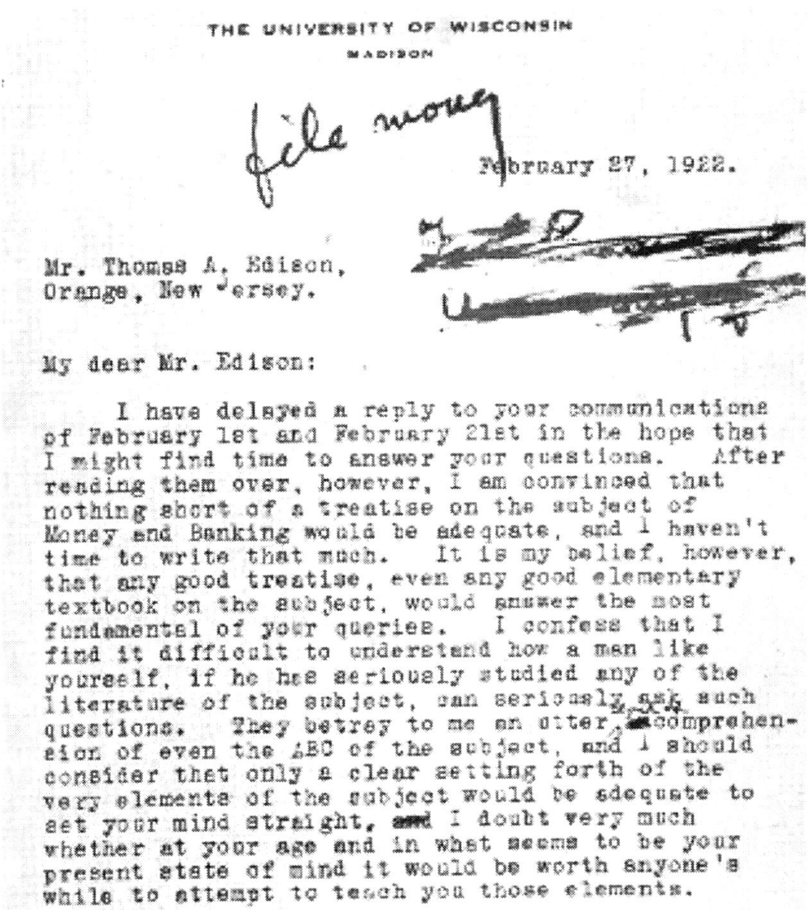

THE UNIVERSITY OF WISCONSIN
MADISON

file money

February 27, 1922.

Mr. Thomas A. Edison,
Orange, New Jersey.

My dear Mr. Edison:

I have delayed a reply to your communications of February 1st and February 21st in the hope that I might find time to answer your questions. After reading them over, however, I am convinced that nothing short of a treatise on the subject of Money and Banking would be adequate, and I haven't time to write that much. It is my belief, however, that any good treatise, even any good elementary textbook on the subject, would answer the most fundamental of your queries. I confess that I find it difficult to understand how a man like yourself, if he has seriously studied any of the literature of the subject, can seriously ask such questions. They betray to me an utter incomprehension of even the ABC of the subject, and I should consider that only a clear setting forth of the very elements of the subject would be adequate to set your mind straight, and I doubt very much whether at your age and in what seems to be your present state of mind it would be worth anyone's while to attempt to teach you those elements.

[162]

Edison lets "Punk" Willis off the research team, but Scott has gone too far. Edison writes a curt letter to the university's president:

[162] February 27, 1922. Banking 1922. TENHP. Reproduced in Hammes and Wills (2004).

March 3, 1922.

President,
University of Wisconsin,
Madison, Wisconsin.

Dear Sir:

Being desirous of obtaining from authentic sources some information on the subject of Money, I prepared a questionnaire and sent it to seventeen Bankers and Economists, asking them if they would kindly answer the questions. Among these seventeen persons was Professor William A. Scott, Director of the Course of Commerce in the University of Wisconsin.

In each case a letter, dated February 1, 1922, accompanied the questionnaire. This was followed by a second letter, dated February 21st. Copies of these two letters are inclosed.

Many of the gentlemen to whom the questionnaire was sent have courteously taken great pains to prepare and send answers to my questions, and others have written stating that their answers are in course of preparation and will be forwarded to me later.

Not so, however, with your Mr. Scott, who has written me a very discourteous letter, not only declining to answer my questions but implying senile decay because of my asking them. For your information I am inclosing a copy of his letter.

Yours very truly,

(Signed) Thos. A. Edison.

[163]

Some in Wisconsin write to Edison apologizing for their rogue professor's poor manners:

> "Many, many people in Madison were shocked when they read the correspondence addressed to you by "Prof." W.A. Scott. There is no one in this city who is in sympathy with him…he appears…to have the idea that he is decidedly IT…now that the matter has been given publicity he may try to reform."[164]

---

[163] Banking 1922, TENHP. Reproduced in Hammes and Wills (2004).

[164] D.E. Mowry, General Secretary, Madison Association of Commerce. Letter to Edison March 23, 1922, Banking 1922. TENHP.

The professor had few supporters, and the public outcry and pressure from administration moves a contrite Scott to write:

THE UNIVERSITY OF WISCONSIN
MADISON

March 14, 1922.

Mr. Thomas A. Edison,
Orange, New Jersey.

My dear Mr. Edison:

President Birge has been good enough to show me a letter from you in which you characterize my communication of February 27 as discourteous. After rereading my letter in connection with yours of February 1 and February 21, I am bound to agree that your characterization was justified, and I hereby offer you my sincere apologies for having written it. I trust that you will destroy it and, if possible, blot it from your memory. I am very sorry that I was so careless as to use language which could possibly be construed as discourteous to a man whose work in his field is so eminent and which I, together with all the world, hold in such high esteem.

Sincerely yours,

Wm. A. Scott.

[165]

With that unpleasantness behind him, Edison set to work analyzing the twelve sets of responses. He surveys them and sees three groups represented. Kemmerer, Patterson, Fisher and Babson are the

[165] Banking 1922. TENHP.

academics; Jay and Harding, the Federal Reserve;[166] and Mitchell, Crennan, Forgan, Kingsley, Baruch, and Kitson the private bankers and businessmen.

Starting with the academics — E.W. Kemmerer, E.M. Patterson, and Irving Fisher — Edison is pleased that they've addressed each of the questions, sometimes at great length.[167] These answers ought to be useful because the academics may have less of a vested interest compared to the others in the existing system. They are not big city bankers. That group Edison suspects will be hostile.

Patterson prefaces his answers by writing that it is difficult conveying one's views to another in brief form, and that

> "...I am anxious not to have you believe that I consider our present monetary system a satisfactory one. It has many very serious weaknesses."

As we saw above Edison thought the second question was "the important one", it is his monetary proposal in a nutshell. So, like him, that is where we will start.[168] He quickly sees, they do not get it. They miss the point.

Patterson, answering numbers 2 and 3 together says that his system:

> "...does not...relieve us entirely from the use of gold...its chief weakness lies in the fact that it proposes a...very unsatisfactory way of supplying the community with a medium of exchange....we shall have a badly adjusted volume of circulating medium...The goods to which you refer would go into storage in largest volume when trade is inactive and when a circulating medium is least needed...stagnation in trade is very seldom, particularly in recent years, due to any lack of volume in circulating medium...this currency...would perform the money functions very poorly, in fact, very much more poorly than does our present system."

Patterson reprises this theme of poorly matched demand and supply of currency leading to large price swings and its inherent inflationary nature repeatedly in answering almost all of the following questions:

---

[166] Again, Jay was the head of the NYFRB, which at the time took its private ownership, autonomy, and influence much more seriously than do any of today's Federal Reserve Banks which appear to be appendages of the Board in Washington, D.C. Harding represented the 'public interest' in his position as head of the Federal Reserve Board, D.C.

[167] Fisher is the exception here. He does not see the actual questionnaire, rather he learns of it through the *New York Times* article of July 16, 1922. He writes to Edison on July 31 requesting more information. They then enter a written and in-person dialogue about Edison's ideas.

[168] Edison's original questionnaire was reproduced by Hammes and Wills (2005b).

"[this plan]...would give us a badly adjusted price level...would give to us an increase in the volume of circulating medium when it was least needed, and give us a smaller volume when a larger volume is most needed..."

"I do not think this could be done without great disturbance....the proposed substitute seems poor."

"Your proposal does not...give a form of money that would be helpful."

Edison sees that he has work to do explaining that farmers need money and have crops — why doesn't Patterson see that? Maybe Kemmerer will see through to the kernel of his idea:

"I do not believe that your plan would provide the mechanism for adjusting the supply of currency to the demands of trade necessary for the maintenance of stability of monetary value...the tendency would be for the public to demand redemption in those goods that were rising in value and to refuse those that were below the value at which deposited; and on the other hand, when it needed more money, to present the particular goods that were tending to be cheap and withhold those that were rising in price. In this way a strong pressure would be exercised in the direction of causing a deterioration in the quality of the commodity reserve. Gresham's law would tend to assert itself by causing the poorer commodities to drive the better ones out of the reserve.

The administrative expenses of the plan would be heavy. The plan I should think would be much more expensive than the Fisher plan and more complicated in its administration....

I think that inflation would result from the plan...largely because I do not believe that it would be politically possible to hold the currency issues down to the basis of the commodity prices...for the period of 25 years you mention.

There would be great danger of increased issues of the money being made under the plea of monetary scarcity, of higher prices abroad, etc. and that once made an endless circle of the type so common in paper money schemes of the kind where the money is backed by land, products...

In my judgment such a money would be exceedingly unsound. It is an example of one of the most dangerous, most frequently advanced and most insidious fallacies of monetary history.

...The so-called Fisher plan offers the best solution of the problem now before the public...The Fisher plan offers a monetary unit whose gold content will vary in such a way as to give a fairly constant purchasing power."

Kemmerer is equally, if not more, critical. Fisher finds more to like in Edison's ideas.

"..the general condemnation which followed your first announcement of as inflationistic was premature. I am very glad you have tried your hand in this matter...[it adds a] powerful stimulation to public opinion which your name always brings, that the imperative of stabilization is better realized...

"...incomplete because of the failure to connect up banking reserves with it, or banking deposits. You cannot stabilize the dollar of money and the dollar of deposits separately as they react on each other."

"I notice you have much the same idea of creating the minimum disturbance of the present system which will still be a step forward."

"[Congressman] Goldsborough...is to have a hearing on this Bill toward the end of August. It occurs to me that you might like to present and express your criticisms...and present your [plan]...My thought is that there is very little chance of any plan being enacted just now but that your presence at the hearing would help enormously to get the public to realize the necessity of some plan and so to get Congress investigating and studying the subject."

"As you...noted...unreasonably opposed...and the bankers rather particularly, to any change and will allege all kinds of fanciful objections — simple mental excuses for opposition. Such foolish unreasonable opposition always yields, however, to pressure."

Fisher's mild encouragement aside, Edison sees that he has even more work to do with the academics. Kemmerer and Patterson certainly miss his mark. These academics may understand some narrow principles, but they miss the big idea.

When he can, Edison relies on his personal persuasive powers illustrated by his interaction with Fisher. Seeing that Fisher misses his mark somewhat, Edison writes:

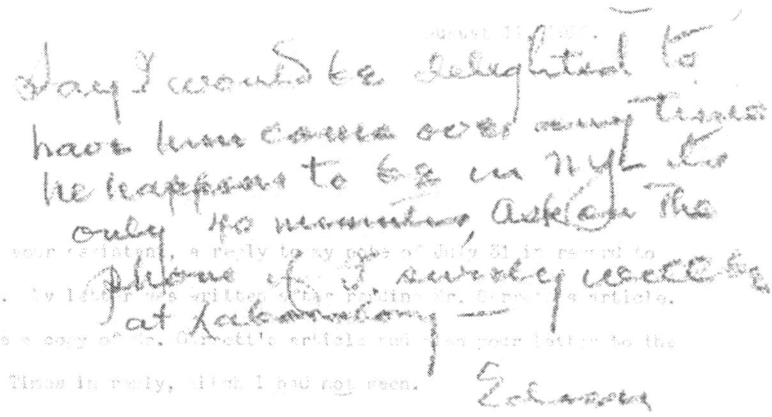

169

Fisher does visit Edison and they discuss much of mutual interest including dietary issues. Edison cannot get Fisher to sign on to his proposal and Fisher can not induce Edison to go to Congress. In response to receiving Fisher's "Stabilizing the Dollar", Edison writes:

"I have read your book...and marked it all up with criticism, some rather severe. You are on the right track, generally speaking, but there are two or three fallacies running through the book and part of the scheme does not have that "brutal practicability" necessary to make it work in the present stage of economic ignorance among the people. Many thanks for the book."[170]

---

[169] On a letter from Fisher to Edison, August 11, 1922, Banking 1922, TENHP. This is characteristic of Edison.

[170] One of the fallacies in Edison's mind is Fisher's reliance on one commodity, gold, to be the standard of value. Edison called this system: "gold illusion" money. The text quote is in Edison to Fisher, December 19, 1922, Banking 1922, TENHP. The "gold

In response to receiving the questionnaire, on March 9, Roger Babson[171] writes:

> "At present, yes, it should be sound money provided the government operated the warehouses to the economic advantage of both producer and consumer...It is possible to answer this question in the affirmative at this time only because the present value of the goods stored and any values we may expect for some time to come will doubtless be higher than the 25-year average which would be taken as a base...The trouble would arise in the industries producing the commodities which are stored. The moment that the exchange values of the commodities taken dropped below the 25 year average we would be compelled to fix or arbitrarily stabilize the prices of these commodities. In other words, we should have to use the particular commodities taken as the basis of value against which to measure all other commodities or services. This would not work out in practice...It is clear, however, that the attempt to use any one group of necessary and important commodities as a basis against which to value other commodities would not be practicable...I also am glad to hear from you and usually I agree with you..."

Edison responds quickly:

> "Friend Babson: You are not in a rut like the eminent economists and bankers who have so far answered my Questionnaire. They have not even understood it. You have not got it quite right."[172]

After considering the mixture of responses from the academics Edison moves on. There are more answers to go through. He'll try the Federal Reserve answers next.

He notes with disappointment that Mr. Jay of the New York Federal Reserve, has kept his response brief. Jay stresses that money creation does not create capital, and it is capital that a nation needs. Secondly, he does admit that a country might be able to get by with

---

illusion" phrase are his words on his copy of Harding's speech cited in Chapter Two. It is my belief that the copy of Fisher's *Stabilizing the Dollar* is somewhere in Edison's magnificent library in the Thomas Edison National Historical Park, West Orange, NJ. It does not appear to be in Banking 1922.

171 April 1, 1922, letter in Banking 1922, TENHP. Babson (see Ahamed (2009), pps. 348-350): was "a well-known market seer...the country's largest purveyor of investment analysis and business forecasts." Given his reliance on charts and tables, state-of-the-art stuff in the 1920s, we would call him a 'technical' analyst today. He also started three business colleges (op. cit, note, pg. 349) and in the late 1920s — contra Fisher — he was predicting the stock market's imminent collapse: the "prophet of loss" (op. cit. pg. 350) or his day's "Dr. Doom".

172 Letter, Edison to Babson, April 8, 1922, Banking 1922, TENHP. This was a holographic letter transmitted from Ft. Myers, FL. Its length and detail causes Edison's assistant William Meadowcroft to write Babson: "Let me say that you are getting something very unusual. I have no[t] known him to write as long a holograph letter as this for more than twenty-five years, and there are very few such extant." Meadowcroft to Babson, Banking 1922, TENHP.

commodity-backed money, but that would end at the borders. An "acceptable standard of value" is necessary to carry on international trade and so far the world has settled on gold.

Edison thinks Jay has missed his points almost entirely. He has not grasped the fact that Edison keeps gold, use that for international trade if you wish. No one is removing it as backing.

Capital? How can farmers build up their farms — build up their capital — if they are getting squeezed off by higher interest payments and lower prices?

Governor Harding is more precise, less encouraging, and to the point. He is not trying to teach Edison anything the way that the academics were.

#2: "I do not think...this would be sound currency..." #3: "I do not think so." "I answer this question (4) in the negative." #5: "Unsound". #6: "I would say yes [over-produce, inflate] to both questions."

The experts are missing the forest for the trees thinks Edison. Part of it is his fault. He just sent them technical questions — maybe that took the focus off the big point. He will have to do the proposal in plain English, provide the blue-print for the people so that they can see its strength and benefits.

With muted enthusiasm he turns to the responses from the private bankers Mitchell, Crennan, Forgan, the insurance man Kingsley, the financier Baruch, and the English industrialist Kitson. He knows that if they find his plan inflationary then this group of people will be heavily against it. This is due to the types of assets and liabilities banks (and insurance companies, too) hold. Their assets are long-term and their liabilities short-term in nature. The assets are government bonds and loans, like mortgages; their liabilities are checking and savings deposits, shorter term.

That means that any inflation lowers the value of the longer term financial assets relative to the shorter term liabilities. Starting from level balance with \$assets = \$liabilities, an inflation causes these companies to go "upside down", owing more than they have, \$assets < \$liabilities. They move towards or into insolvency. They may go broke. Inflation is a 'financial fire' scarring their balance sheets and potentially putting them out of business entirely.

"Sunny Charlie" Mitchell, president of the country's largest bank, provides twenty-seven pages on the history of money and sixteen more pages on the questions.[173]

[173] Note that the "history" section is *not* provided in the Appendix.

Q2: "[T]he plan...would lack elasticity – responsiveness to fluctuating demands ... great expansion in the fall, then continuous contraction ... great pressure on Congress to enlarge the list of eligible commodities ...the plan is inferior to the system in use now..."

Q6: "There might be rapid inflation in the Fall and enforced and drastic contraction during the remainder of the year, with an inadequate supply in the Spring...As the basis of a monetary system the plan seems to us incomplete and inadequate in every respect.

Q16: "...there is no more demoralizing influence upon the community than irredeemable issues of paper money."

Q26: Suggests that inflation has outpaced wages in Germany leading to a falling real wage, thus giving Germany a cost advantage over other countries. This is unsustainable..." The German people do not view the depreciation of their money as a subject of congratulation."

It is no better with Crennan: "Of schemes to set up substitutes for gold money, there have been no end. These projects...have been exposed as fallacious time and again."

Forgan, a banker from Chicago, is slightly less pessimistic:

Q2: Your plan "...would be as sound as National bank notes secured by Government bonds; but like them, might lack the elasticity which our present Federal Reserve notes enjoy. They would not as readily respond to the fluctuating commercial demand for them."

Q6: "There would be no undue inflation...except to the extent that it might remain in circulation after the 50% loan...has been paid and the merchandise disposed of and consumed...the farmers would have no inducement to "over-produce so as to stock up on currency."

Q15: Leave a gold standard? "Not under any system so far proposed that has come to my attention."

Q26: Germany. "When the crash comes, the chances are that the pensioners, widows, and orphans, who are dependent upon an inelastic income, will be the worst sufferers."

On to Kingsley. He puts words to some of the frustrations that Weston, Willis, and Scott must have felt:

"...your questions are generally hypothetical, resting on assumptions which are frequently in direct conflict with human experience. Serious answers to such questions are not only difficult but dangerous to the respondent.

Take, for example, your first and eleventh questions. You might almost as well ask me what would happen on the Planet Jupiter if, within our universe, the laws of gravitation should cease to operate. If I undertook to answer that question and a lot of other men did the same thing, you could, with some plausibility, conclude that we disagreed amongst ourselves as to the laws of gravitation.

I have, because of my admiration for you, proceeded on the theory that you are really seeking information. It has not been easy to maintain this attitude as your ideas are old and have been repeatedly tested with disastrous results."

Q2: "No; such paper would not be sound money…its administration would be incalculably expensive. It would not be issued to satisfy the demands of business, which is the real function of money. It would result in enormous inflation…would work vast injury…to the capitalist…and most certainly…all those whole sole capital is labor in some form."

Q5: "There is small choice in rotten apples."

Q6: "It is fundamentally a plan to inflate the currency—to inflate it enormously."

Q7: "The whole plan would probably smash things so quickly that it is useless to draw any analogies."

Q10: "Such currency would not be sound money."

Q13: " "Money" that rests on goods, materials, even real estate, is not sound money. The "wit of man" long since learned that. Of course the lessons of history mean little to the men who call all history 'bunk'"

Q15: "No."

Q26: "Germany is working…because she is beaten, because she is hungry, and because of the hectic stimulus of excessive inflation…the middle class has been wiped out…she will probably go to smash…we shall work out to prosperity largely because we have not abandoned our standards — and one of these is the gold standard.."

Edison turned to a real capitalist, Bernard Baruch.

"One day I received a call….Edison was on his way over to see me at my home…When he arrived he told me that, having heard of my interest in the farm problem, he wanted my views on a plan for credit and marketing which he had drafted at the suggestion of his friend, Henry Ford." [174]

The men discussed Edison's plan, with Baruch later writing Edison:[175]

"First, let me say that your thoughts along this line paralleled mine to the extent of using the warehouse graded and insured product as the basis. The only difference…you go direct to the Federal Reserve Bank for the issuing of money without interest for 50%...whereas I furnish a financing corporation, which will lend to the

[174] Baruch (1960), page 158. Baruch was a "Wall Streeter" who advised Presidents including Wilson and later went to Washington, D.C., and served in the F.D. Roosevelt administration.

[175] Baruch to Edison, May 26, 1922, Banking 1922, TENHP.

farmer, say 70% or 80% of the then-going market price of his commodity...You go direct to the farmer without interest...

Mr. Garrett and I both agree that the basis of the issuing of the money is correct in principle. The only question is its application. If wisely administered and limited, with the proper check upon it, I can not see any weakness in your plan...

But I do think it is unnecessary and undue favoritism to let the farmer have the money without interest. Nor do I think it fair to limit the number of commodities...

...see the farmers and get their reaction upon it. I do not think they will like it...In closing let me congratulate you upon the directness with which you went at this subject."

Edison was pleased, now he was breaking through, and to a Wall Streeter no less. Yet, Baruch still could not clear his mind of the interest 'Devil' and he wanted limitless commodities included. That would not work.[176]

"Friend Barcuh [sic]: Thanks for your letter. You are the first man who has had the imagination enough to throw off the trammels of the money religion and analyze the proposed scheme like an engineer. After you have thought it over more I think we will agree more fully."

Baruch was "highly complimented" by Edison's response, but the exchange on this topic seems to have ended there.[177]

Finally Kitson. Being an industrialist, it is not clear that he is as anti-inflationary as the above bankers and insurance men (barring Baruch). Businesses sometimes owe more money, to suppliers and to laborers, than they are owed. If the prices they receive for their goods rises and they can pay back loans in 'cheaper dollars', then maybe they come out ahead.[178]

Kitson jumps in to the Questionnaire with relish (italics in the original):

---

176 Edison to Baruch, May 29, 1922, Banking 1922, TENHP.

177 Baruch (1960), page 158.

178 Kitson received the questionnaire (returned it March 3, 1922, Banking 1922, TENHP) thanks to a correspondence with S.P. Panton of Billings, MT. Panton was in the second group of seventeen to receive the questionnaire requesting it from Edison in a letter dated January 17, 1922, (Banking 1922, TENHP). In Kitson, Edison finds a kindred spirit. Kitson is an inventor and manufacturer of industrial and locomotive lights, the Kitson lamp being one of his inventions. He also spent time in the U.S. in the late 1800s and knew of the monetary issues of that day. He publishes several books on monetary issues. In England he spoke before the parliamentary Cunliffe Committee in 1918 predicting woe for England should it return to the gold standard. Fisher knows his work and refers to him. He was known as an "inflationist" and was noticed by no less than J.M. Keynes as one of his "great Trinity of crankdom" along with Peddie and Douglas (Skidelsky 1995, page 416). For more on Kitson and his monetary thought, see Hammes-Wills (2005b).

Q2 & Q3: "Money so issued would be more secure than if gold were behind it…money…based upon *the credit of the Government* has behind it not merely the gold in a country but *all the wealth of that country including gold*, hence the Government bank note should be regarded as a far greater security than one issued by a banker against one commodity — whether it be gold, silver or pig iron."

Q7: "The present danger of an over-issue of currency is the increase in the prices of commodities. The could be easily remedied by the Government fixing prices of all commodities…an over-issue of currency under such conditions could not affect prices and therefore could do no harm."

Q9: "The value of currency depends not upon what it is made of nor what it is backed by but upon the number of units in circulation."

Q13: "In my judgment the public are not interested in what is behind money, all they want to know is whether it is legal tender and will satisfy creditors."

Q17: "Every great moral teacher from the time of Moses to that of John Ruskin has condemned usury (interest) as one of the greatest evils in national economy. It has been forbidden by every religion."

Edison's head spun. He asked specific questions because he had faith in his over-all plan, but wanted to know about specific parts of it. His experts, from the academics — with (almost) nothing at stake — to the bankers and insurance men, found the specifics and the over-all plan deficient. True, Fisher thought it had potential, but was he encouraging plans 'farther out' than his own so that his would look conservative and safe in comparison? After all, his plan kept gold as the only commodity backing money and he was no friend to the interest-free loans.

Baruch was mildly positive, but he, too, was pushing his own warehouse scheme, and he did not see the check on commodities nor the banning of interest as important to the farmer. Edison was not letting the interest Devil in to his plan!

Kitson, now he was fully on board…maybe a little too extremely so. Fixing prices? Edison knew that it was the price level one wanted to stabilize, not fix every price. Individual prices are, and should be, determined by supply and demand. He'd written that to several people setting them right after they mistook his ideas:

"Prices have nothing to do with my endeavors. Prices are subject to supply and demand, even when our money is 100% good and abundant in quantity."

"Prices should only vary by reason of supply and demand and not have additional variation due to doubts as to the purchasing power of the money itself."

"…prices will then be those which arise from supply and demand." [179]

---

[179] Edison to I. Ludlow, New York City, April 24, 1922; Edison to W.B. Johnston, Kansas City, MO, July 27, 1922; Edison to M.K. Graham, Graham, TX, April 20, 1922. All letters in Banking 1922, TENHP.

Edison also believed that Kitson was wrong about eliminating backing commodities. Nothing at all anchoring the price level, how would that work?

Various phrases pinged through his mind. "Fallacious", "Old ideas", "inelastic" currency "failing to meet the demands of trade", "expensive to administer", "highly inflationary", "subject to political pressure, manipulation, and abuse", "damaging to capital and labor", "sends the system to 'smash'". Most of them, especially the original 'research team' may as well have called him 'Kaiser Bill' given the death and destruction they said his system would cause. The verdict from the "research team plus four" was grim.

Well, perhaps not so disappointing if one is Thomas Edison. Used to negative results, remember finding out "10,000 ways something won't work" is not failure, he wrote: "For instance, take my question No. 2. Not one of these men [bankers and economists] understood this question."[180] So, maybe his plan was not faulty, the readers just did not understand the question being asked. Edison relied on research teams to do the tedious 'grunt' work. He found them valuable in the process, but they were just part of the larger process. He did not always yield his own insights and inspirations to their findings.

However, in the context of the entire list of twenty-six questions across the respondents, it is hard, unless one is very self-confident, which Edison was, to conclude that they misunderstood what was being asked. Yet, that is what Edison did, concluding: "Any man who has been ten years in banking [and economics?] is unable to see a new thing clearly. He's in a rut."[181] So, almost by definition, he concludes that he has chosen the wrong research team.

More importantly, Edison is finding that he has an ace-in-the-hole: the American people. He was hearing from the farmers and their families. The very people, half the country, he is trying to help. He also heard from the *New York Times.* They wanted to do a lengthy, exhaustive, article on his proposal. It was to be written by Garet Garrett, a very skilled financial writer and a close friend of Baruch's.[182] This would be Edison's chance to go over the 'experts' directly to the people, as Baruch himself suggested, and have them read about his plan in his words. The people would not let him down.

---

[180] Letter. Edison to Hugh W. Sanford, of Knoxville, TN, March 8, 1922; Banking 1922, TENHP. By that point he'd received all but Weston's and Jay's responses.

[181] *New York Times*, Section Seven, page 1, July 16, 1922.

[182] Baruch (1960), pages 2 and 233.

CHAPTER 10: A MAN, THE PLAN, AND THE *TIMES*

"If a system of checks can be worked out, and I think it can, the farmer will get justice. He has been robbed by the East for over 100 years." (a)

"Financing a farmer is far more difficult for a bank than financing a manufacturer; yet I do not believe the farmer has ever had a fair show for one-half a century." (b)[183]

The word that 'Edison's working on a plan to stabilize the dollar and help farmers' had been out since his brief visit to Muscle Shoals. Content that people knew he was working for them, he was hoping to keep the details of his plan under lock and key. He felt blindsided when the questionnaire leaked out; why, it got out before he even received the responses from his experts.

Once out, he started receiving letters from around the country. Depending on what they had read, details of his plan were sketchy to non-existent.

"...I take the liberty of again suggesting that you should put a full statement of your plan before the public at the earliest possible opportunity... It is the newspapers rather than Congressional Committees that make public opinion and the editors and financial writers who have only a partial knowledge of your proposal are damming it in advance, and unless you anticipate them they may kill the child before it is born. I was in Washington on Friday and found that some of the salient features of your scheme are already known but I has not yet been put before the public in its entirety."[184]

In turn, Edison used farm correspondents to inform him of how their businesses worked in practice. Did elevators and operators take unfair advantage of them? If so how? He wrote brief letters to country newspapers requesting that their readers send him information.

"...he desires to obtain all of this kind of information you can give him, especially as to how the banks break the farmer. He also wishes to ascertain the facts about elevator charges and the action of the speculators in the grading of wheat. He is particularly interested to learn just how it is done, and whether there is a charge, in grading, for the graders to get a "rake off." (a)

"He says that he knows of the abuses which you mention, but what he needs is a lot of facts...what are the things that you do, say, from the barn to the railways station, to the

---

[183] (a) Edison to A.W. Rings, Mayetta, KS, May 9, 1922; (b) Edison to George Roberts, V.P., National City Bank, New York City, March 14, 1922; both letters in Banking 1922, TENHP.

[184] Theodore Price, Editor, *Commerce and Finance*, New York City, to Edison, May 29, 1922; Banking 1922, TENHP. On this copy Edison has written, "Tell him in a few days—."

elevator, etc. Hos(sic) the price ascertained? Who grades and cleans the wheat? What are the charges?...Is there a change of cheating on grading?" (b)[185]

This network was a second set of 'experts', not in money, but in the actual practice of financing and marketing a crop. The main message from the farmers — as we've seen — is that they needed an orderly marketing system, 'honest' grading of their crops, and a reasonable rate of return.

Edison also played the grand, wise old man in Washington, D.C. He was very comfortable corresponding and visiting with Senators and cabinet Secretaries, trying to influence their legislation. Being Edison, he could not be publicly ignored. Yet, polite as they all were, everyone wondered, 'Where is his plan?' Parts of it leaked with the questionnaire in late February 1922, but readers had to infer copious missing details. He wrote and spoke as if there was a well worked out plan, but where and what was it?

As more of his ideas coalesced, Edison started to give out details to correspondents in April and May. John S. Wannamaker — the South Carolina cotton farmer and president of the American Cotton Association — received a detailed frequently-asked-questions, or 'FAQ' letter from Edison dated May 12, 1922. At the same time, Edison was working on the full version of the Proposal (for the final version see Appendix) doing a revision on May 13.[186] The Proposal was still not ready for 'prime time' — but answers to the FAQs, were starting to come out.

Writing on May 12, 1922:

"Dear Mr. Wannamaker,

I fear that the gentleman whom you sent to me may not have fully understood my general idea in its entirety and, therefore, might unconsciously have conveyed a wrong impression. So I send you herewith a simple illustration of the principle involved. This is only for your own personal information. Please do not let it get out, as I am merely trying to help the Farmer through those who are working hard to help him. I would prefer no publicity.

As to the warehousing, I have a plan all worked out, so that if you could get a Bill put through, this plan could take care of the whole of the coming crop without any expense to either the Government or to others.

Yours very truly, (*signed*) Thomas A. Edison"

---

185 (a) Edison to A.W. Rings, Mayetta, KS, April 20, 1922; (b) Edison to C.P Bump, West-Logan Farmers Union, Clay Co., NB, April 27, 1922; both letters in Banking 1922, TENHP. I think that the word "change" in both letters was intended to be "chance"...the bottoms of both have: WHM:FTR...Meadowcroft to ?

186 FAQ letter: Banking 1922, TENHP. This letter followed a conversation Edison had in Washington, D.C. with a Col. Harvie Jordan, the national secretary of the American Cotton Association. A typescript version of the Proposal, headed "Revise May 13, 1922" is in Banking 1922, TENHP.

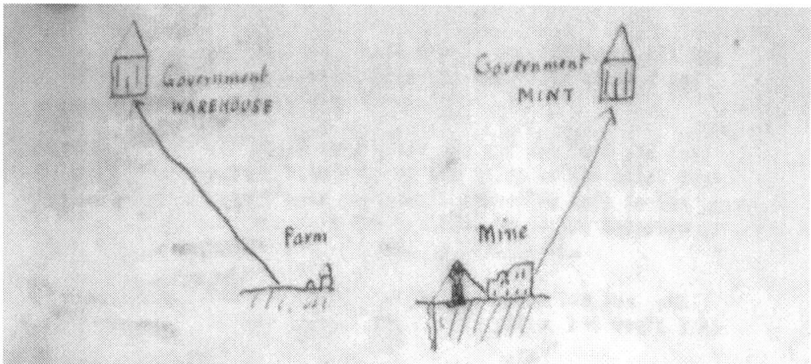

Gold miner brings his commodity to the Mint. It is graded, and he receives its full value in gold certificates and pays no interest. Costs Government nothing except expense of printing the paper certificate. The Government does not charge the miner anything for grading because it is so anxious to get this commodity that it foregoes this charge.

"The farmer takes 10 bales of cotton to a Government Warehouse, where it is graded. He asks for the issuance of a certificate and then wants the government to loan him money on the certificate. The Government says we cannot loan you the full amount that you can get for it if you sell now, but we find that the average price of your cotton on a gold basis for the last 25 years is 20¢ per poud [sic]. This is our method of appraising values [with the handwritten "Illustration" here]. So you mortgage your cotton and we will loan you 50% of the appraised value in Federal Reserve notes — the same kind that we print and furnish to the bankers for merchandising commodities.

You understand, Mr. Farmer, that you cannot have unlimited storage rights. We will only give one year to remove all your cotton. You must sell a percentage every month over the whole period, otherwise some of you farmers might try to hold your cotton and get a higher price and if this failed it might result in confusing the public who buy your cotton.

Farmer: I have 10 bales of cotton and a certificate; how am I to sell a bale every month or so over the whole year?

Government: When your 10 bales are graded, you will get 10 certificates. – Our unit is 1 bale of cotton. When we have wheat the unit is 100 bushels. Hence, you can come to the warehouse, hand in the money we loaned you on it and remove the cotton. Or you can sell your certificate on the Exchange, or to anybody, and the purchaser will bring it to us together with the money loaned and we will deliver the cotton to him.

Farmer: Do I have to sign my name to anything?

Government: No, we do not require names; we only loan on cotton in our possession, graded and appraised by us.

Farmer: But suppose I sold a bale and had spent all the money received from the loan, how could I get the bale out?

Government: You could not. After you got the loan you have parted with some of the value of the bale. Your certificate represents the value left in the bale. You can sell the certificate on the Exchange or to Bankers, subject to mortgage.

Farmer: But suppose I thought the price too low, and wanted to hold for higher price, how would I do it?

Government: Well, we have loaned you one-half the money on your whole crop. That removes your immediate wants and we give you a whole year to market and sell the balance, but we will not permit you to hold the whole of your cotton and sell it at any time in one lot. This would open the doors to outside speculators and would also confuse your customers. You must know that we have other farmers to look after, and all the men who buy the cotton, wheat and other commodities of the farmer. Almost any banker will loan on your first certificate because he likes short loans.

Farmer: Suppose I wanted to sell all my 10 bales within a month after storing them when I thought the price was good?

Government: You can do that at any time. Our rules prevent you holding your crop because you are not satisfied with the price. We give you a fair chance to hold and market over a year, and not glut the market when all of you must have money. We take care of that when we loan you one-half of the whole value at the start. A month after you get this money you may not want to sell the first of your 10 bales because you then have plenty of money from the loan and perhaps because the market price is not satisfactory, but you will have to do so. Your average price of your 10 bales over the whole year will even up matters for you.

Farmer: What do you charge us for doing all this when you say we do not have to pay any interest?

Government: We charge you for grading, storage and a small charge on the cost of the Warehouses, to wipe out the cost in forty years. This will be less than what you have always paid. The Government is not doing this for profit; it is doing it so that it can be truly said it exists to actually serve the interests of the people who created it, not theoretically but practically."

The letter is more than the rough outline provided in the questionnaire and patiently explains Edison's view of the system in operation.[187] The farmer could take his crop to one of twelve government-owned, but privately operated warehouses. Ultimately, he foresaw more than 1400 of these warehouses across the country.[188]

---

[187] It is unstated, but understood that farmers would not have to participate in this program if they chose not. However, if they did, these were the rules. See *The Proposal* in the Appendix for all the details as released by Edison.

[188] "You are mistaken in thinking my plan contemplates Government marketing. I have avoided in every way any Government operations [of the warehouses]." Edison to A.S. Goss, Washington State Grange, Seattle, WA, December 21, 1922; on the number of warehouses, Edison to W.B. Johnston, Kansas City, MO, July 27, 1922; both in Banking 1922, TENHP.

"The warehouses are to be built gradually over a period of years and by money received from taxation. The warehousing charges include depreciation and 5% interest on the cost of warehouse and handling machinery."[189]

Farmers receive fifty percent of the value of the crop in Federal Reserve notes, the nation's money. This is newly created money. Farmers do not have to sell their crops in to a falling market. The value is determined by the average price of the crop over the past twenty-five years. The crop can be stored in the warehouse up to one year. The farmer also receives equity (ownership) certificates to the crop. These come in standardized units and are marketable at any time on "the exchanges," the commodities markets.[190] The crop stored in the warehouse has to be brought to market — at a minimum — of 1/12th of the amount stored per month. If not, the government will sell that amount of the stored crop 'for' the farmer. This is a check on speculation.

In order to get the crop out of the warehouse, the owner of the certificate, which may be the original farmer or whoever buys the equity certificate on the exchanges, pays back the money given the farmer. This cancels out the money created at the time of storage.

Orderly marketing. Interest-free money. Self-canceling money. Money, that for every new dollar circulating, has fully two dollars of commodities backing it. What's not to like? Edison was convinced that he had solved several problems at once: the farmers' being held hostage to big city bankers' actions; viciously cycling farm prices; speculative manipulation of prices, grading, and warehousing; money, whose value could not be counted on from one year to the next.

He was so sure that on June 1, 1922, he wrote U.S. Senator Arthur Capper:

"Friend Capper:

I see...you are going for the Exchanges...in [my] warehouse system...no speculator would dare to sell short or for future delivery. It would be too risky...I think these Exchanges can be made a benefit to the farmer...I have read of these bodies[Exchanges] for over a period of three centuries, and every attempt to stop them has been disastrous to all. The only way is to steer things so they become a benefit.

I hope no legislation will be made along the Warehouse line until I get a scheme to fight out the Plan given you. People are commencing to understand [my] Plan more and more...I have an answer good and sufficient for every objection...

If once this general Plan is first put in operation in a small way, requiring but little money I feel sure it will extend over the whole United States in a few years and

[189] Edison to Babson, April 6, 1922, Banking 1922, TENHP.

[190] These are American call options, see Hammes and Wills (2006). Edison knew options: "I understand the difference between cash and option markets for commodities, as I use them myself." Edison to George T. McDermott, Topeka, KS, April 26, 1922.

divorce agriculture entirely from manufacturing and commercial banking."[191] *(Emphasis added.)*

The midnight oil had been burned, the experts—academic, business, banking and farmers — consulted. All that remained in the campaign was for the plan to be splashed across the national media — the *New York Times.* Edison had turned down several requests from regional media for interviews, he was saving that for the *Times.* Edison would explain the plan to the *Times'* Mr. Garrett. He would write it up, and the rising tide of approval should wash it right through the halls of Congress.

Edison wanted to be clear and precise. Many wrong ideas and misimpressions about his plan were floating about. He knew from the experts' responses that it came across as "greenbackism" and inflationary. If they could not interpret his question No. 2 correctly, how could the average newspaper editor? Edison also felt an obligation to many others in explaining an augmented monetary system with clarity.

Once it was out that he was working on the problem literally scores of people wrote him with their monetary ideas. Some included examples of proposed or actually operating alternative monetary systems, as evidenced on the following page.

From Minneapolis there was the "Payday Dollar", which was an interest bearing note:

[192]

[191] Banking, 1922. Capper, from Kansas, was the point man in the U.S. Senate for farm legislation. Edison visited him in Washington, D.C. from time to time keeping an eye on legislative matters.

[192] This and successive images from Banking, 1922, TENHP.

From Oregon, a "merchant dollar":

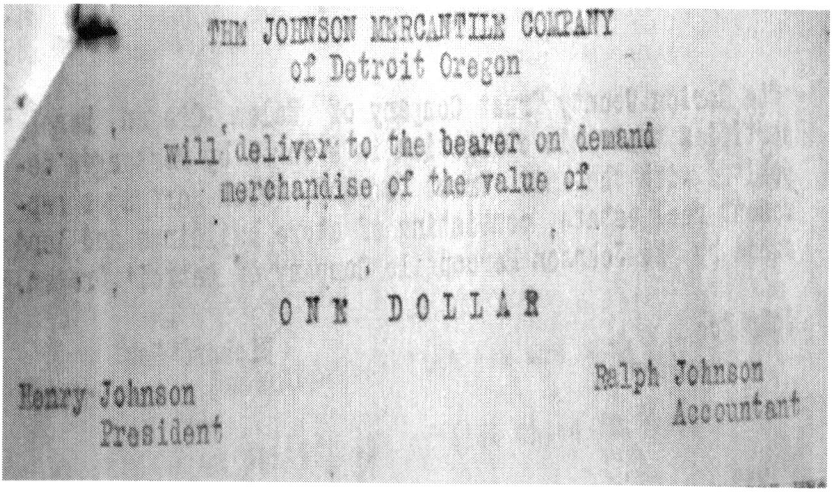
THE JOHNSON MERCANTILE COMPANY
of Detroit Oregon

will deliver to the bearer on demand
merchandise of the value of

ONE DOLLAR

Henry Johnson
President

Ralph Johnson
Accountant

From Alabama, the cotton warehouse receipt 'money':

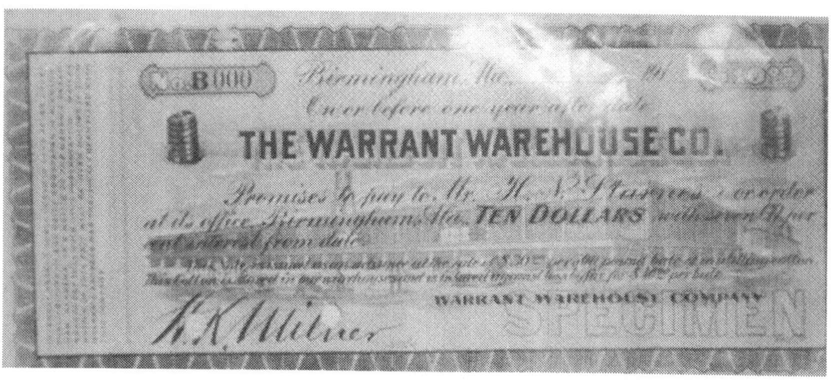
THE WARRANT WAREHOUSE CO.

TEN DOLLARS

WARRANT WAREHOUSE COMPANY

SPECIMEN

There were more, but without the warrants, coupons, and notes attached. Were these the 'bitcoin' of their day? Idaho's "aluminum" money; monetary plans from Vancouver, Canada; the "industrial" dollar, Washington, D.C.; Chapin, Colorado; the dollar plan backed by "patriotism" from Houston, Texas, the 'labor dollar', other schemes from Los Angeles, and Kansas City, Missouri. He did not put much faith in any of these, but inspiration and right-thinking could come from anywhere.[193]

He knew that local areas had often experimented with their own currencies. Their weaknesses included that they did not always have well-defined purchasing power, were not readily accepted outside of their local area, nor were they good for international exchange. By grafting on to gold, and not abandoning it, he thought his plan had better features and shared the same underlying motivations. He felt he was speaking for many, not just himself.

Edison and Garrett had several pleasant conversations. Edison found that Garrett was penetrating and a careful listener. He was no stranger to Wall Street nor to questions of money.[194] But Garrett was no pushover, either. While respectful, did Edison see a little glint of doubt in his eye? Was their a tone of skepticism in his voice?

The *New York Times* spared nothing. Headlined "Edison's Idea for a New Kind of Money", including the flattering illustration and inlaid boxed section on "the Monetary Sayings of Thomas A. Edison," they gave Garrett the entire first page and one-third of the second in a special section of the Sunday paper, July 16, 1922.[195] Edison was pleased.

In the article Garrett reflected Edison's process and thoughts with care. The warehouses, the fifty-percent mortgage certificate, convertible in to Federal Reserve currency—paper money—at the farmer's bank, and equity certificates, the self-canceling nature of the money as the crops are removed in an orderly way from the warehouse. The value of two times the money created held in commodities. The article flows freely, unburdened by quotes. These are in the boxed section and they sum up his feelings nicely:

> "I want to cast the variable out of money." "Stability! That's what we want. There's no gain from instability except for the speculators — and what happens to them?" "I don't believe there is any such thing as Money Power. There is the power of money."

---

[193] No doubt due to its similarity to his plan and to its apparent success, he was intrigued by the warehouse scheme from Birmingham, Alabama. It had apparently been used successfully in 1914. The 'money' was backed by warehoused cotton. Once Edison heard about this scheme, in a letter from Charles F. Wood, V.P., Warrant Export & Discount Corporation, Birmingham, Alabama, dated July 20, 1922, he sent letters and examples to many people, including "Friend Capper" (July 31, 1922). Banking 1922, TENHP.

[194] In 1911 he authored a penetrating look at Wall Street, *Where the Money Grows*, Harper and Brothers.

[195] Helpfully, one-third of the second page was given over to a related article: "Depreciated Money Problem in Europe" on the rampant inflations in Europe—variable and unstable currencies! *New York Times*, Special Section, page 2, July 16, 1922.

"When I propose to issue money against the basic necessaries of life, up to only half their average value for a quarter of a century, the financial editor of a New York paper says: 'Why, that's fiat money.' Well, billions of money are now issued against commercial paper, Liberty bonds and Stock Exchange collateral, impalpable things you can't eat or wear. What's that? He's in a rut."

"All new things about money and banking, all the great reforms, come from outside. I find that in the books." "This gold money is not good enough. It's a fiction." "In all the books on banking and economics I read how stupid and disastrous it was for the Government to have done this and that in a crisis. I never find out from them what the Government should have done." Edison is telling them.

"Agriculture and manufacturing cannot be financed by the same method. Their needs are too dissimilar. The farmer has one turnover. Business has many." "We ought to do something about the farmer. It's a moral obligation. He doesn't know anything about the figures. He gets skinned."[196]

Garrett ends that article with a brief section on Edison's ignoring of the bank credit situation. Many feel that the alternate expansion and contraction in bank credit causes the wild price gyrations—just as Edison saw on the 'test-bench'. When asked, Edison replies:

"I know that myself. One thing at a time. Let's make money itself absolutely sound as the first step. Then the credit problem can be taken up. That is a vast problem. I can't do anything with it in my mind — not yet. I put that aside."

It's an odd way to end the story, Edison thinks. Yes, he'd like to solve the bank credit part of the money complex. But, solving the farmers' problem and making money sound, shouldn't that be enough for now?

Wait, what's this? Half, if not more of the total page space, is given over to "A Discussion of the Edison Money Plan," It is no discussion. It is Garrett's opinion. He is critical and he is blunt:

"The idea of warehouse money is very old...[the two checks on money expansion] (a) That storage shall be for one year only, and (b) that the amount of money issued upon a given commodity shall not exceed one-half of what has been its average value for a period of twenty-five years...would be subject to mutilation by political interference...Mr. Edison does not account for the fact that a monetary system must function in a political atmosphere amid the passions of conflicting self-interest."

He defends the gold standard as providing an external control on the amount of money and bank credit that can be issued:

"What gives gold its unique merit as the base of money is precisely the fact that it is a fetich, universally recognized, to which people react irrationally in a manner that ultimately serves rational ends."[197]

---

[196] All from *New York Times*, July 16, 1922, Special Section, page one.

[197] 'Fetich' in this usage means: an object that is believed to have magical or spiritual powers.

"The fantastic output of paper money against a vanishing ratio of gold is what makes the price of a newspaper 1,000 rubles in Moscow and the price of a pair of shoes several hundred marks in Berlin. It was the enormous increase in paper money and bank credit in the country between 1914 and 1920 that caused prices to more than double.

"Mr. Edison sees this. But his mind declines to deal with it. The subject is too vast, he says."

"What will limit the commodities defined as 'essential goods' that can be brought to the warehouse? Mr. Edison's arbitrarily chosen list?"

"Who shall have the power to say what the limit of money must be? Mr. Edison? Congress, with its farm bloc in strife with an industrial bloc?

That is what the gold standard is for. Less and less does gold perform the function of money [medium of exchange] at all. More and more its function is to limit the creation of paper money and bank credit.

This fact is very important and needful to be expounded, because the world is running after money fallacies with a new zest and the true function of gold is not clearly perceived."

That all the wealth changing hands in the world should be priced in relation to a quantity of yellow metal...may seem barbaric. But it is an arrangement that serves as no other arrangement yet thought of would equally serve to control the issuers of paper money and bank credit.

Bankers cannot be trusted to issue credit in their own direction. Governments cannot be trusted to issue paper money on good intentions. They must all be restrained by a gold reserve.

What people complain of is not that prices are high or low, but that they rise and fall. And this is owing but remotely, hardly at all, to changes in the supply of gold. The great price fluctuations of the last few years were caused by the failure of the world to keep its output of paper money and bank credit within the bounds of gold.

There will be no way to test [Edison's plan], no way to see whether it fluctuates or not, no way to tell if it is better or worse than gold money..."[198]

Edison reads this with resigned sadness, but little surprise. If the experts did not understand his plan, why should Garrett? One need hardly say it, he is in a rut! But, even Edison had to realize that he, too, had become immersed, "I've been thinking on the subject steadily for several months. Maybe I'm in a rut."

In the same issue the *Times* ran a polite editorial suggesting that 'new money' was not the answer to the farmer's dilemma. If they know nothing about numbers, they should be taught numbers rather than "provided a newfangled money or to allow them to make over the

---

[198] All quoted material from "Discussion of the Edison Money Plan", pages one and two, Special Section, *New York Times*, July 16, 1922.

banks or the exchanges."[199] Well, that's not it, Edison grumbled. It is not new money, newfangled or not. It is the same money made stable.

Edison wrote a short rebuttal, saying in part: "Mr. Garrett...although an extremely able man, has not got my scheme entirely right in his mind... Somebody will someday evolve a plan, so I thought I would at least make a stab at it."[200]

Garrett had made a good point or two. But, Edison had not used one of his favorite analogies describing what he was trying to achieve. It sure helped him organize his thoughts. This was the 'poker chip' analogy. This analogy illustrated the trading-playing process. When poker players start a game "...they select the banker, he takes their money and gives them the chips. When they stop playing they don't want a lot of I.O.U in the pot."[201] "...the Federal Reserve notes or other notes are the poker chips of commerce. In practice we do 185 billions of business on 6 billions of Federal Reserve notes, or poker chips. If these chips are secured by the deposit of actual commodities having twice their value they will always be good.[202]

"I have not touched credit money, etc. I seek only to have our poker chips always redeemable, and a plan in which there can never be inserted any false values in the currency to disturb prices. Prices should only vary by reason of supply and demand and not have an additional variation due to doubts as to the purchasing power of money itself.[203]

"If the players are reckless, and the play is high, and most of them ruin themselves, I am not concerned. That is quite a different thing. But the chips or currency with which they play the game of business must always be redeemable in real wealth. This removes one variable, but the other variables are many and the excessive manufacture of credit is the worst."[204]

Maybe that would have helped Garrett and the others. Players who pay five dollars for a five-dollar chip, want that chip to be redeemable for five dollars at the end of the game...no I.O.Us. If the chip is redeemable for five dollars, then the real value of the chip is maintained. Sure, a player may lose chips to others during the game ('ruin himself'), but whatever chips he does have are redeemable at the same rate he paid for them. He does not find at the end of the game that his five dollar chip has sunk to three dollars.

---

[199] *New York Times*, July 16, 1922, page E5. A short response by bankers was critical of the plan, *New York Times*, July 18, 1922, page 27; two letters to the editor, *New York Times*, July 23, 1922, page 91, were also polite yet critical of Edison's plan.

[200] Published on July 23, 1922, *New York Times*, page 34.

[201] Undated, handwritten, notes in Banking 1922, TENHP.

[202] Letter to W.B. Johnston, Kansas City, MO, July 24, 1922, Banking 1922, TENHP.

[203] Letter to W.B. Johnston, Kansas City, MO, July 27, 1922, Banking 1922, TENHP.

[204] Letter to Thomas Joyce, Washington, D.C., July 24, 1922, Banking 1922, TENHP.

What he thought he saw in the economy was farmers paying five dollars in commodities for a 'poker chip' (Federal Reserve note) and later in the 'game' when the farmer redeemed his 'chip' it did not buy the same amount of commodities. No banker in a poker game could get away with that. The farmer's chip had a variable value and he wanted to 'cast out the variable'.

This would have to wait. Edison passed his hand through his hair and shook his head; he'd given this money complex a thorough study. Maybe he was in a rut. Writing to Irving Fisher (August 7, 1922):

"[I] did this for Mr. Ford and [am] not highly interested in urging it, but [I] think in years to come people will come around to [my] view.",

to "Friend Capper":

"As time goes on you will find that more people will understand the Plan I submitted, and it will be the basis of our currency within thirty years. (June 2, 1923, Banking 1923, TENHP)

Ty William Trufant Foster:

"I would like to go into further explanation, but cannot just now because I am so very busy."[205]

and to M.K. Graham:

"Nobody seems to realize the difference between currency based on our present system and that based on a mortgage of rapidly moving commodities that are necessary for life. Hence, I am through with this subject and no longer have any interest in it."[206]

Besides, he'd neglected the businesses. The business that had grown so much through the years that in addition to the manufacturing plant in Orange, it had spun off what was to become General Electric with factories in Schenectady, NY, employing over 18,000 workers. He had to get back to improving the phonograph, business machines, batteries, and cement. On the side he'd think on Ford's rubber question. There was no end to problems needing solutions!

Edison was letting the farmers go further into the 1920s without him. Were they to remain ignorant of numbers and continue getting "skinned"? Every now and again Edison cast an eye to the newspapers to see what progress was being made.

---

[205] Foster, an economist, with his colleague Waddill Catchings criticized the Edison plan in the popular magazine, the *Saturday Evening Post*, December 23, 1922; also in an address before the American Academy of Political Science, November 23, 1922, and in their book *Money* (1924).

[206] Edison to Fisher, August 7, 1922; Edison to M.K. Graham, April 30, 1924. Banking 1922 and Banking 1924, TENHP.

As he personally knew, Senator Capper and the ubiquitous Herbert Hoover were working on plans for farm relief when he was meeting with them in May 1922.[207] In July of 1922 Capper shares Hoover's relief plans with Edison. Hoover's plans revolve around changing the Federal Reserve Act to enable Federal Reserve District banks to make loans to 'main street' banks using farm loans as collateral.[208] This represents a significant change in the intent and purpose of the "real bills" operating philosophy of the Fed. It is the first known instance of Federal Reserve *quantitative easing*. In this case, practiced through an expansion of what is acceptable collateral at the Fed's discount window. Expanding the collateral from factory-manufacturing loans to farm loans as well. [209]

Post-war rebuilding, stabilizing of markets and international trade patterns, and resumption of business-as-'normal' also increased demand for farm output and farm prices rebounded.[210] Real average net income per farm doubled between 1921 and 1925, though the migration from the rural to urban areas was not staunched.

Finally, the Federal government's fiscal policy aided economic activity. While the Federal government continued to run budget surpluses all through the 1920s, which would be considered tight or contractionary, how can an economy expand when the government reduces expenditures? The other side of fiscal policy, taxation, stimulated growth. Under Treasury Secretary Mellon, the federal government dramatically reformed the income tax structure to lower tax rates. As a result: "Income tax receipts rose during the 1920s, in part because incomes rose, but also because it was no longer worth avoiding taxes [due to the lower rates]. In 1921 the income tax yielded $719 million from 6.6 million returns; in 1929 the tax yield was $1 billion from four million returns."[211]

---

[207] June 9, 1923, Capper writes Edison: "My dear Friend: Your letter of June 2 received. I have read your plan for amendment of the federal reserve banking system with the greatest interest…I doubt very much whether we can get anything like it through the next Congress…I want to discuss this and other suggestions for helping the farmer with other members of the Farm Bloc…". Banking 1923, TENHP. So, legislatively Edison's plan appears dead. However, the Farm Bloc was just gathering strength. This era and the early 1920s depression in particular, marked the rise of out-sized political power for farmers. Power that would last until the 1960s. See Hansen (1991).

[208] Hoover to Capper, July 19, 1922, Banking 1922, TENHP.

[209] This was the Agricultural Credit Act, passed in early 1923, amending section 13 of the Federal Reserve Act, allowing agricultural paper of up to nine months' maturity to be eligible for rediscount at Federal Reserve District banks. See Harding (1925) pps. 222, 238-245.

[210] Some crops and products assisted by some tariff protection from the Emergency Tariff of 1921.

[211] "Supply Side" tax-cuts. See Atack, J., and Passell, P., (1994), pps. 576-577.

National unemployment rates were sliced in half between 1921 and 1923, fluctuating between four and five percent through the remainder of the decade.[212] The decade was now roaring.

Edison's plan, relying less on gold and more on other anchors, the ones he thought would ultimately prevail, once people cleared their eyes of the illusionary shine from the golden metal, seemed dead. Or, was it? In about a decade, gold would be under attack as the basis for the world's financial system. Individual's ownership of monetary gold would be declared illegal — illegal! — in the U.S., the gold parity ratio of $20.67 to the ounce would be arbitrarily changed to $35 to the ounce and the nation's monetary system would be vastly different than any of the so-called experts predicted in 1922.[213] Gold was effectively gone as an anchor. Unconceivable to the experts! Going forward there was nothing but the restraint of the Federal Reserve to anchor money.

Had he lived, the old inventor would have no doubt remembered the 'experts' gold-blinded, sometimes scornful reproaches to his questionnaire with a bit of a chuckle if not outright laughter. Who needed the teachings of the ABCs of money now? Their allegiance to gold, blinded them. 'They were in a rut after all and the good ideas do come from the outside!'[214]

---

212 Smiley, G., *The U.S. Economy in the 1920s*, http://eh.net/encyclopedia/article/smiley.1920s.final

213 Presidential Executive Order 6102, April 5, 1933. Modified by EO 6260 and 6261; the Gold Reserve Act of 1934.

214 Edison died October 18, 1931.

CHAPTER 11: WAS EDISON RIGHT AFTER ALL?

What of Edison's plan? Did it make any sense? It probably lacked the "practicability" he had hoped for and it did seem ripe for manipulation. It did have major flaws and these were pointed out at length by the experts, including Garrett.

As they noted, it most certainly would have been subject to political manipulation. No doubt there would have been immense pressure to lengthen the list of thirty-six original crops (#14, see "A Proposed Amendment" for the list) to include just about every 'productive' activity that could be somehow 'warehoused' interest-free. (Including storage on disks? In the cloud?)

Undoubtedly there would have been pressure to raise the up-front fifty percent pay-out to some higher percentage. The immediate pay-out of fifty percent of the twenty-five year average price for a crop represented a guaranteed price floor, so naturally, those receiving it would like it to be greater. Those not getting the same deal from the government, would wonder — loudly — why not? The price floor also represented government price-setting in those cases where the current market price was below the twenty-five year average. How popular would government price-fixing have been?

The price floor worked as follows. Suppose wheat has sold for $2 a bushel each year for the last twenty-five years. Its twenty-five year average price is $2 a bushel. If, for some reason, the price of wheat in year #26 is $0.50 a bushel, a farmer depositing wheat at the government's warehouse immediately receives $1 per bushel, fifty-percent of the twenty-five year average price. The farmer can never do worse than this $1 per bushel. Why should farmers of certain crops be extended this guaranteed price floor *and* interest-free loans?

The infusion of money as crops were put in to storage and the cancellation of money as crops left storage would probably have added to price swings, not moderated them (as Edison hoped), as the experts noted.

Operating over 1400 warehouses (though Edison did want to start modestly with twelve) would have been very costly. Who knows if even 1400 would be a sufficient number? Edison did try to put checks on cost in place having these privately operated and government regulated, but the taxpayer was the ultimate risk-taker in the scheme.

The equity certificate would have made the farmer a speculator in ways that Edison, trying to protect the farmer from risk, may not have appreciated. However, unlike earlier work (Hammes and Wills, 2006) where it was surmised Edison did not fully appreciate this speculative element, newly found correspondence makes it clear that he was fully aware of it. For example, he wrote to Roger Babson, (April 8, 1922, Banking 1922, TENHP):

> "4. Another illustration. Suppose a farmer puts in the warehouse 1000 bushels of wheat...The average price for 25 years...is $1.20 per bushel. The farmer is given $600 [1000 x $1.20 = $1200; and 50% of $1200 = $600]...
>
> He then can hold his wheat by means of his [equity] certificate until he thinks the price is satisfactory and thus be independent of the speculators who now set the price ahead months before the crop is reaped [so, the farmer is the speculator!].
>
> This certificate is bought on the exchange at the market price. Now say $1.36 for wheat. The farmer would get $760 [1000 x $1.36 = $1360, minus $600 = $760] as the wheat is higher than the 25-year average.
>
> If on the other hand it was selling at 96 cents he would only get $360 [1000 x $0.96 = $960, minus $600 = $360]...the capacity or possibility of fluctuation is entirely transferred to the [equity] certificate which is subject to the prices due to supply and demand."

In Edison's example, the farmer always gets $600, then depending on the market price, he will get some additional amount, in his example, anywhere from $360 to $760 extra. Edison sees this as *a certain* $600 plus either $360 or $760. Yet, the equity certificate may fluctuate in value from $360 to $760.

Rather than seeing this as a variable $960 to $1360, Edison breaks it down into constituent parts with all of the variability placed on the amount derived from sales of the equity certificate. It depends on one's point of view. The alternative views are: variable, with a realized value between $960 to $1360, or a certain $600 with an additional variable value between $360 and $760? Which is better for the farmer? Are they different? Edison thought so.

He noted that if wheat sold for 59 cents then the equity certificate would be valueless. Let's see; 1000x$0.59=$590, but it costs $600 to get the wheat from storage, so the equity certificate is worth about minus $10.

It is clear that Edison is fully aware that the farmer has speculative opportunities and, as we saw above. Edison is fully aware and expects that these certificates will trade on the existing commodities exchanges. But to protect the farmer, as noted above, he also provides certainty for the farmer: the worst that the farmer can do — the price floor — is set by the twenty-five year average price which is known before planting. For those to whom this 'service' was unavailable would undoubtedly feel bitter and discriminated against.

What about the gold miners, did they have such a privileged position as Edison thought? Remember, Edison thought that they got full value for their gold from the mint. But, the miner's dilemma was that the price of their product was arbitrarily fixed, in 1922 at $20.67 per ounce. What happened when prices of other goods rose? Why, gold miners lost out. Suppose wheat is $1 per bushel, then, the prices given, one ounce of gold is equivalent to 20.67 bushels of wheat. But, if wheat prices double (which they more than did in the 1915-1920 period) then gold drops in purchasing power from 20.67 bushels per ounce of gold to 10.33 bushels per ounce. It may not be profitable to keep mining. Shut the mines![215]

This interplay between the purchasing power of the dollar and prices was noted by Edison and he asked Babson to do a chart for him (May 1, 1922, Banking 1922).

"I note that the new crop cotton is 18 cents. It would make a very interesting curve to plot the average selling price of cotton from 1914 to 1921. I think it would make it more interesting to add to the same sheet, as near as possible, the average index purchasing power of money, to get the real price of cotton or other commodities."

Babson did the chart (Banking, 1922, TENHP):

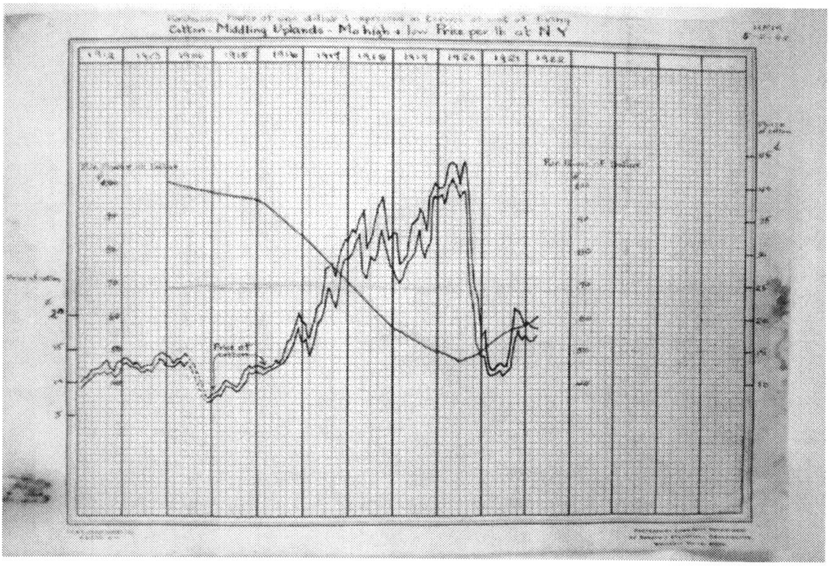

The jagged lines show the nominal (or current dollar) price of cotton per pound, the solid, downward-then upward sloping line is the purchasing power of money. Falling between 1915 to 1920 when there was price inflation, then rising when there was price deflation. What it shows is that the falling purchasing power of the dollar was offset by rising cotton prices. Later, in 1920-1922, when cotton prices fell, the purchasing power of money was rising, and that partially offset the farmers' losses. Babson noted this.

The result, as Babson wrote (May 3, 1922, Banking 1922):

[215] This, in fact, is what happened in that period of rising prices and what happens today when gold prices fall below their cost of production.

"I have charted the data which you suggested and enclose record. It certainly is very illuminating and should serve as fine evidence indorsing your position... I am almost converted!"

On this letter Edison wrote: "Many thanks, from your curve the real price of cotton was about 25 cents, yet it varied from 8 cents to 43 cents [in nominal — or sticker price — terms]. How the people are fooled."[216] It is this sort of variability Edison is trying to 'cast out' of money.

So, Edison and the experts, both were 'wrong'. Edison was right that gold need not be the sole anchor of the monetary system, but wrong in proposing *more* commodities be added as 'anchors'. If one anchor is a 'relic', are many less so? His plan certainly would create a cumbersome, costly, monetary mechanism just to give farmers a hand-out. Through the subsequent years the Farm Bloc and its legislators (e.g. Capper) figured out many different ways to accomplish that goal without interfering with the monetary system.

This may explain Edison's failure to gather support for his plan in the halls of Congress. Politicians, like Capper, were unfailingly polite when he met with them, but they saw easier — and more direct — ways to help the farmer with targeted legislation.

Through the years, farmers won (and sometimes later lost) price-support policies, price-parity support programs, land bank programs, explicit crop subsidies, tariff support, and subsidized loan programs.[217] Federal government departments, especially Agriculture and Commerce, led in the Harding administration by the contentious, often-sparring, and empire-building Henry C. Wallace and Herbert Hoover, respectively, sought to gain additional power and influence through appeals to farmers, farm groups, and agricultural interests.[218]

This attention and direct legislative success reduced pressure on Edison to 'help the farmer'. Analytically, as cumbersome and favor-granting as Edison's plan was, the monetary 'experts' did not do much better. They could not see past gold's glitter. 'Gold illusion' as Edison would say. Within a few years gold was, for all practical purposes, eliminated from the nation's monetary system. It was illegal for a private

216 On May 6, 1922, Edison passed along this information to Wannamaker, writing: "The farmers everywhere, and not alone the farmers but all people not knowing the laws of money, naturally thought they were highly prosperous [when farm commodities prices rose] and on that basis contracted debts. These debts were contracted on low value money and will have to be paid in money of greater value." Banking, 1922, TENHP.

217 See Hansen (1991).

218 Hawley, E.W. (ed.), 1982, Herbert Hoover as Secretary of Commerce: studies in New Era thought and practice, Hoover Presidential Library Association, University of Iowa Press.

citizen to own monetary gold! What expert predicted that? What was left in its wake? The nation's central bank, the Federal Reserve System and the anchor was the Fed's attention to the price level.

The Federal Reserve and its policies have been carefully examined by many, including most thoroughly by Milton Friedman and Anna Schwartz.[219] As an institution it did not perform very well in most episodes of national economic distress. Cause and effect? Many have argued that it was poor performance by the Fed which led to economic distress. There were Fed 'puts' (low interest rates) and Fed 'calls' (high interest rates) causing the money supply, prices, and interest rates to gyrate leading to swings in employment and unemployment. It has been noted that the Fed sometime seems to exacerbate cycles rather than being able to counter and dampen them; thus, it has added to economic instability not stability.[220]

Perhaps the Fed can be excused for imperfect tinkering with the level and rate of growth of the money supply, but it has also been accused of allowing hundreds and thousands of 'main street' banks and their credit-facilitating roles to fail during both the 1920s and the 1930s. This weakened the financial system at the 'main street' level and made most people much worse off.

Why would the Fed do that? The twelve Federal Reserve District Banks are owned by their member, commercial, banks. If non-member banks fail, that reduces competition for the member banks. Isn't it also a sign of 'bad management' if a bank chose to not become a member? These attitudes seemed to prevail within the Fed in the 1920s and 1930s.[221]

While there may have been a narrow self-interested defense of this policy, the public goods aspect of banking apparently escaped the 1920s Fed. If your (non-member) bank fails, I may become more worried about my bank's safety, even if it is a member bank. Most likely I don't even know its membership status. All I see is your failed bank,

---

[219] See their *A Monetary History of the United States*, 1867-1960.

[220] This problem of being pro-cyclical has been studied as part of the "rules vs. discretion" problem. A 'monetary rule' has been shown — in some circumstances — to dominate discretionary policy. Of course, the gold standard is one type of rule, but it is not the only one. Gold 'rules' are expensive and waste resources. A country has to have gold on hand for monetary purposes meaning it cannot be used for other purposes. That was a problem with Edison's plan, too, where he advocated ton upon ton of foodstuffs would be stored away, some of it lost to waste and decay, rather than being consumed. Modern rules, when they are in place, rely on a stated policy: 'price stability', or having the price level or money supply grow by a certain percentage annually, rather than having a resource-wasting gold anchor. For overviews see: Buol, J.J. and Vaughan, M.D. (2003); Van Lear, W. (2000).

[221] Friedman and Schwartz (1963), pps. 357 and 358. The Fed no longer discriminates against non-member banks when making discount loans.

your sad face — if you lost your deposit — and I do not want the same thing happening to me. I might run down to my bank and withdraw my funds. If enough people are like me this creates financial difficulties for my bank and it may fail for lack of funds.[222] Bank failures prevented lenders and borrowers from getting together as easily. Economic activity was further squelched and unemployment rose.

This is part of the Federal Reserve history that the current Chairman of its Board of Governors, Ben Bernanke, knows so well. That is why the current Federal Reserve has been so active and aggressive in providing substantial financial support in the form of lending to, and buying troubled assets from, the financial system. This support has even extended beyond what have traditionally been considered financial institutions and banks.

In 1934 the Roosevelt administration removed gold as a national anchor for the money supply; it prohibited private citizens from redeeming their paper money for gold. They even prohibited the ownership of monetary gold. They did leave gold as an international anchor with the U.S. government buying and selling gold with other governments at $35 to the ounce.

The Bretton Woods Agreement at the end of World War II pegged currencies against the U.S. dollar and the dollar to gold at $35 to the ounce. Again, private citizens could not ask to redeem paper money for gold, but foreign governments could. In the early 1970s, as the U.S. started to print more paper dollars, some of which flowed overseas, foreign governments presented more of these dollars for redemption at $35 per ounce. The U.S. government was running out of gold at $35 to the ounce. In response, the Nixon government broke with the Bretton Woods Agreement slamming shut the 'gold window'. Since then, there has been no international anchor for the dollar. The only anchor has been the skill and motivation of the Fed.[223]

How has it done? The next figure shows the value of the dollar starting in 1970 at 100. It is measured in terms of two standards: all consumer goods and services and gold. In terms of goods and services the purchasing power of the dollar has fallen from 100 in 1970 to 17 in 2011. In terms of gold, the purchasing power of the dollar has fallen from 100 to two (2) in 2011.[224] What thundering speeches might we

[222] Federal deposit insurance was not introduced until 1933/1934. Approximately 10,000 banks failed between 1927 and 1933. See Walter, 2005.

[223] See Hammes-Wills, 2005a.

[224] Sources:
http://www.minneapolisfed.org/community_education/teacher/calc/hist1800.cfm (consumer prices) and http://www.measuringworth.com/datasets/gold/result.php (gold). Accessed August 4, 2011. The reader can see that purchasing power has fallen

have heard along the banks of the Tennessee River if Edison had experienced that?

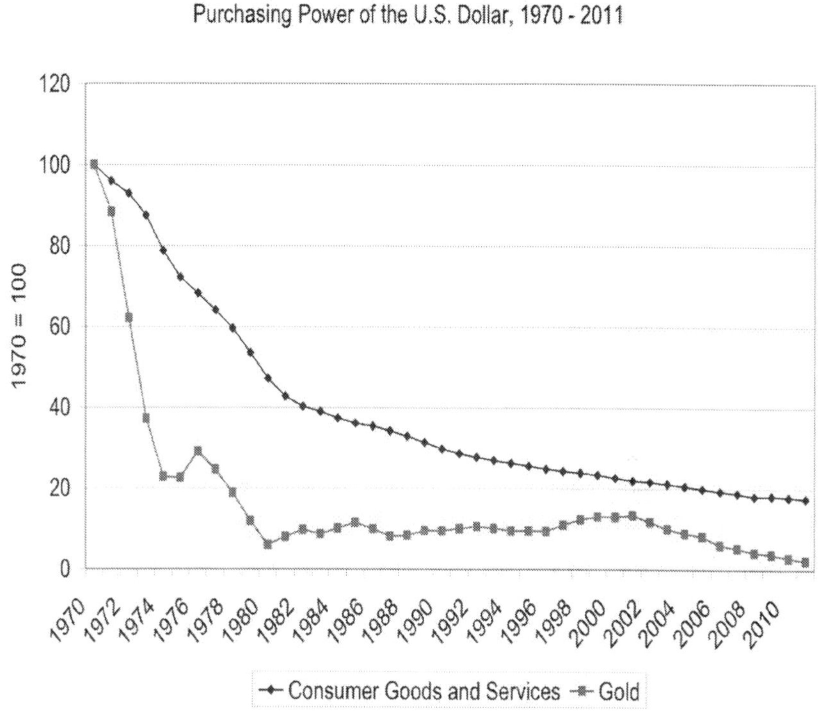

If one looks at the purchasing power of gold (in terms of how many units of goods and services it can purchase) then one observes since 1970 — shown in the next figure — a very bumpy ride.

Since 2002, the purchasing power of gold has risen by a factor of four. But, from 1980 to 1985, the value of gold relative to goods and services plummeted. Gold does not always "rule." What does this say about the Federal Reserve as an anchor for the purchasing power of the U.S. dollar? It is no surprise that in times of a variable dollar that substitutes and competitors arise. Trading clubs, 'Bitcoin', foreign currencies, commodities, all start to look better as stores of value when the value of our unbacked paper money fluctuates unpredictably. Rather than 'casting out the variable' out of paper money, we cast out the paper money and move to what we hope will be more predictable substitutes, as illustrated:

more regularly relative to goods and services than gold. Similar charts for the period 1800 to 2011 are provided in the Appendix.

One Unit of Gold Buys This Many Units of Goods, U.S.

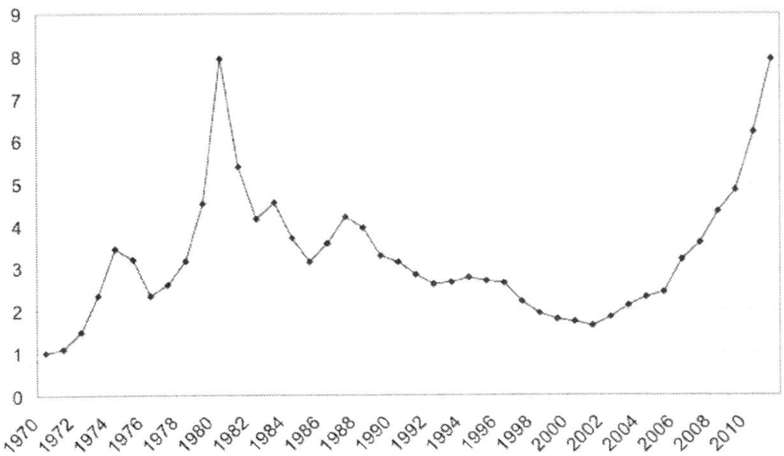

So the loss of an arbitrary, well known, anchor like gold in the absence of a binding rule on behavior may allow for monetary laxity and poor economic performance. In fact, from *assignats* to Continentals, to Greenbacks to Reichsmarks in the 1920s, that is exactly what we have seen episodically through history. Yet adherence to gold (or any anchor) may prevent discretionary — just-in-time — moves which may enhance short run economic performance.[225] Do we want something like a sudden gold outflow to cause a decrease in the money supply, a drop in prices, and debt-deflation recession? Wouldn't we like a bunch of smart people managing money to offset that looming disaster?

If Edison's plan could be accused of being manipulated for political purposes, what about the current monetary system? Is the Federal Reserve an Olympian actor, public-spirited, above politics, and immune from political pressure managing money optimally? Of course, what history has shown, is that careful, smart, people still cannot be trusted to manage money to stabilize its purchasing power.

Take a look at the Fed's current balance sheet.[226] The Fed is holding about $2.9 Trillion worth of 'financial assets' on its balance sheet. Think of its balance sheet as its 'warehouse'. About $1.6 trillion are U.S. Treasury bonds and $1 trillion are mortgage-backed securities (MBS) and other assets bought from distressed U.S. financial institutions in 2008 and 2009. In the past the Fed held, or warehoused, U.S.

[225] This, at least, is the argument from the Federal Reserve.

[226] As of July 28, 2011. A balance sheet shows the assets and liabilities. Assets are those items the Fed has chosen to buy and hold. Typically, its liabilities—what it used to pay for the assets—are part of the money supply chain.

Treasury bonds almost exclusively. In the recent financial crisis it chose to expand its asset portfolio and add MBS 'assets' and make loans.

Now their balance sheet includes these MBS created by private financial institutions and which were termed "toxic assets" (or even worse) in 2008-2009. The Fed bought these and (in effect) gave the financial institutions newly printed paper money. No one really knows how the price was determined. Maybe the Fed used the average of their price over the past twenty-five years? No one really knows.

Wait! If the mortgage-backed securities were put in bushel baskets and those bankers dressed in overalls, it would look like Edison's scheme! True, financial institutions are not farms and bankers are not farmers, but they did sow and reap these MBS, receive a pay-out (50%, 100%?) for their 'crop' of "toxic assets" and that 'crop' is being stored by the Fed. The financial firms are holding on to the paper money (bank reserves) and the Fed is even *paying* interest on the money that they paid for the toxic assets! The Fed took all the risk out of the MBS assets. That's even more extreme than Edison's zero-interest scheme to help the farmer. Imagine if Edison had suggested that the government warehouse should pay interest TO the farmer for storing his crops! Edison got the 'crop' wrong, but he got the scheme right — as he said: his was a plan that would be in place within thirty years. Make that ninety years, Tom.[227]

So, what sort of monetary system do we have and how does it relate, if at all to Edison's scheme? Is there knowledge in Edison's scheme that might lead to monetary stability as we move forward. Is there a hidden 'truth' in Edison's plan (as some would argue there is in Nostradamus or ancient Maya writings) that will guide us through the future? Will knowledge of Edison's plan at least allow us, as Santayana hoped, to not re-live history?

As we have seen, Edison was more than a crank, knocking about in unfamiliar territory. He was right to wonder about reliance on gold, and right to think that some credible limit — a check as he termed it — on money creation was necessary to achieve a money with stable purchasing power. Would his plan have created that credible limit? Probably not. The experts were likely right. His plan also promised a complexity of operation, opportunities for political manipulation, and costs that would have been prohibitive. However, his experts did strike-out in their allegiance to gold. Like Edison's plan, gold too was gone in a few short years.

Is what we have today a plan with more certainty surrounding the purchasing power of money? Today we have the Federal Reserve

---

[227] Also missing in the current scheme is any sort of known, orderly, marketing plan to divest the MBS from the Fed's balance sheet. The paper money may never self-cancel.

System responsible for ensuring the purchasing power of our money. How have they been doing? Not very well if the evidence shown in the graphs above is to be believed.

Of course, the Federal Reserve might respond: "You do not know how bad it might have been if we had not been there." That response means that we have to take it as a matter of faith that they have successfully responded to economic problems and offset them, not exacerbated them. It depends on one's faith, but there is little in the history of the Federal Reserve that makes one believe that they focus only on the economic factors and stay above the political wrangling. Thus, they may add to the political 'business cycle' and instabilities introduced when short run re-election outcomes dominate long run economic outcomes.[228]

The attractiveness of an automatic, impersonal, no-favorites, monetary mechanism like the classical gold standard sends its charms to us like the sirens of Greek mythology. But, is it fool-and tamper-proof? Not when governments can — and have — arbitrarily re-set gold values, from $15 per ounce of gold to $20.67 per ounce of gold to $35 per ounce of gold to…Each of those re-settings means significant and dramatic losses of the dollar's purchasing power.

Nor is current Federal Reserve policy 'automatic' in any sense of the word. Therefore, to remove arbitrary and political considerations, some have argued for constitutional rules or simpler operational rules to restrain Federal Reserve policy. Simple rules like "Set the rate of growth of the money supply to equal the long run rate of growth of output" take short run, politically-oriented, considerations out of the policy makers' weaponry.[229] Yet, in times of economic distress, which are likely to bang in to our economy from time to time, do we want a major economic policy-maker to sit still claiming their 'hands are tied'?

Edison's plan is long gone. Or, is it? However, his question is still the right one to ask. Has, or can, an unconstrained Federal Reserve System (or any central bank) manage to find the checks and balances, while avoiding the political pressures, to provide long-term price stability? Has the Federal Reserve — or any central bank — truly cast the variable out of money?[230]

---

[228] See Meltzer (2003), and *Inside the Nixon Administration-The Secret Diary of Arthur Burns, 1969-1974*, (2010) edited by Robert H. Ferrell.

[229] This view, sometimes adjusted for some minor factors, is most often associated with Milton Friedman, Milton Friedman (1960), *A Program for Monetary Stability* (New York: Fordham University Press).

[230] The search for answers continues, e.g., see the essays in Dorn, J.A. and Schwartz, A.J. (1983). See also essays in Bordo, 1999. Rolnick and Weber (1997) provide evidence that under *fiat* money standards, inflation is higher than under commodity standards.

APPENDIX: EDISON'S ORIGINAL PROPOSAL

The following pages display a reproduced photocopy of Thomas Edison's original Proposed Amendment to the Federal Reserve Banking System:

A Proposed Amendment

to the

Federal Reserve Banking System

Some time ago Mr. Ford asked me to see if I could not invent some plan for helping the Farmer. I have approached the matter in the same way that I do with a mechanical or other invention, namely, get all the facts as far as possible, and then see what can be done to solve the problem.

The development of this proposition has been made in two parts, namely, "The Plan" and "Notes." In the latter I have made a few observations about the amendment proposed and also a few disjointed remarks about money.

THOMAS A. EDISON

Orange, N. J.

THE PLAN

1

The Government of the United States might establish sectional concrete warehouses, equipped with the most modern machinery for handling, loading, unloading and grading; and, in addition, provided with an automatic sprinkler system to reduce any damage to the stored contents due to the action of fire.

2

The plans of such warehouses shall be obtained by public competition. These warehouses shall consist of an administrative section and a power station. Added to this nucleus are the storage sections. At first, one or two sections are to be constructed. Provision should be made for the erection of additional sections so that the entire plant will be sufficient to warehouse all the permissible commodities which may probably be offered from the area in which the warehouse is to serve.

3

All such warehouses to be built by contractors in open competition, the Government guaranteeing the contractor against any unforeseen physical obstacle not known at the letting of the contract; all work to be done under inspection of Government engineers and checked by Travelling Inspectors. Three-fourths of the actual money expended, after certification by the Government Engineer, to be paid to the contractors each month for the work done in the previous month.

NOTE: Guaranteeing against unforseen obstacles and the monthly payment will insure low prices for construction.

4

These warehouses are to be constructed of reinforced concrete poured in forms. The Government will furnish the steel forms into which the concrete is to be poured, and also all the necessary machinery of the most approved and latest character for handling forms and concrete, for which it will make no charge to the contractor. The contractor, however, is to be responsible for any breakage of, or injury to, such forms or machinery that may occur while carrying out his contract. These contracts shall contain the usual provisions and guarantees as to the financial and technical ability of the contractor to carry out his agreement.

5

Congress to authorize, at first, the building of six one-section warehouses in the cotton states and six one-section warehouses in the wheat states. These to be operated over a satisfactory period of time and to form the nucleus of a very extensive creation of Government warehouses throughout the United States—adapted and used for the storage of approved necessities of life for limited periods of time.

6

No commodities are to be allowed storage facilities beyond a period of one season. Any commodity not removed at the expiration of this period may be sold at auction, or by tender, or otherwise, at the option of the Government. The proceeds, after deducting what is due to the Government, to be placed in a National Bank, subject to the claims of the original owner.

7

The administration of the warehouses to be under a single Government Officer appointed under Civil Service rules and held entirely responsible for the working of the warehouse. The actual physical operation of the warehouse is to be carried out through a contractor obtained by open bid, such contract to last for one year only. Each year new bids must be made. The contractor not to be incorporated. The bills of the contractor, after approval by the Government

4

official in charge, shall be paid monthly. The clerical labor necessary for administration shall be let out to public auditing concerns by competitive bids; the salaries and expenses to be paid monthly in the same manner as the contractor.

8

All such warehouses are to be located at the most favorable points for shipment by railroad, or water, or both, and room provided to add sections of warehouses to meet all reasonable future requirements in the area served.

9

The Government is to form a company which shall operate these warehouses. All the stock of such company should be owned by the Government. The object of this is to create a legal personage or defendant that may be sued in a Federal Court, should any person have a claim that for any reason requires adjudication.

10

The money to build these warehouses is to be raised by taxation. The price to be charged for storage is to be on a universal basis for everyone, and to be made up of four items, viz.:

1. Actual cost of loading, unloading, grading, etc.

2. Allowance for depreciation on warehouse machinery, etc.

3. Insurance.

4. An extra charge to form a sinking fund to return cost of construction.

11

The entire operation of these warehouses should be closely inspected, as to quantities and kinds of commodities graded, by Travelling Government Inspectors, under the control of the Treasury Department at Washington, or a Government Commission. The

5

Accounting Department shall undergo the same scrutiny by ample inspection.

12

Upon receipt of any commodity, and after proper weighing, a preliminary receipt for the same is to be given. It is then to be manipulated, or graded, and three sets of sealed samples taken; one being given to the owner and two being kept by the Government. The Government will thereupon issue a receipt in duplicate for the commodity; one receipt setting forth the quantity and grade of the commodity. The other recites the same thing, and, in addition, gives the holder the right to receive in Federal Reserve currency, at any National Bank he may choose, 50 per cent of the average value of the commodity as determined by the prices over a period of 25 years, without any charge, other than cost of service and a contribution to the sinking fund. For this the bank may make a definite charge for obtaining the currency from the District Reserve Bank. The duplicate receipt is kept by the owner and contains his equity over and above the loan of 50 per cent. This duplicate is available for a loan at a National Bank or it may be sold on the Exchanges, or held by the farmer until he desires to sell. Both certificates may be split up in fractions at the pleasure of the administration.

13

After twelve preliminary warehouses for cotton and wheat have been built and operated, and the plan is found satisfactory for building up a safe basis for our money system, the twelve cotton and wheat warehouses can be extended by adding more storage units already provided for in the original plan, and other warehouses can also be built in desirable areas to accept other commodities for storage and the issuance of loans thereon. In addition, warehouses belonging to private concerns may be bought, if fireproof and capable of being operated economically.

6

14

The following commodities may probably be acceptable:

Cotton, wheat, barley, rye, hay, oats, buckwheat, flaxseed, flax, rice, American sugar, cloverseed, wool, peanuts, onions, soy and lima beans, cow peas, Porto Rico coffee, linseed, linen, almonds, English walnuts, pecans, cheese, tallow, lard, hams, bacon, rosin, bituminous coal, prunes, dried apples, dried apricots, raisins, degerminated corn.

As our experience increases other articles could be added should the requirements of our expanding business require a greater amount of base commodities, and the farmer requires more storage accommodations.

15

All commodities to be eligible for storage must originate in the United States or its dependencies, and must be subject to storage *and* mortgage, and not for storage only.

NOTES

A. In the administration of this system it might add to the conveience of the farmer, purchaser, exchange or bank, to have all commodities standardized as to quantities, or units, like stock certificates; the usual stock certificate unit being for 100 shares. In like manner, 100 bushels might be the standard unit adopted for wheat, etc., where such products are measured in bushels, or that equivalent in metric measurements.

B. The Federal Reserve money so issued on a warehouse commodity will buy and is exchangeable at all times for any other commodity in the warehouse as far as the loan is concerned. All the variation as to prices is relegated entirely to the equity certificate, the price of commodities varying according to supply and demand, in some cases, and, in other cases, to an impairment of the value of the currency through an excessive sale of doubtful credit.

C. Should bituminous coal be given storage it would cure a great evil, by giving continuous work to the miner. This would give the miner a much larger yearly income at a very much lower wage, thus greatly cheapening the cost of coal. It would insure the railroad and industries of an even supply of coal and serve to prevent to a great extent the periodic disturbances we now have, as the Government would control the situation by the storage of 150 million tons, and prevent many bad features in mining, which go towards waste and overproduction of coal. Bituminous coal cannot be stored properly except under water as it gradually loses its gaseous combustible matter and is very liable to catch fire spontaneously.

D. Coal storage pits 1,000 ft. long and perhaps 80 ft. wide, 20 ft. deep, could be dug with sloping banks to the angle of quiescence, and the sides and bottom lined with concrete. There might be a double track on each side, with two or more cranes provided with clam shell buckets for loading into cars. For unloading into the pits a travelling crane, with track, could carry the cars as received from the mines and dump them into the pits. It would only be necessary to have a few Government Officials in each district and a chemical laboratory to grade the coal, with checking inspectors travelling from one storage area to the other and frequently changed.

All operating should be done by contractors by bid. Fifty per cent of the average cost of coal of the same qualities in the different areas, ascertained as substantially correct over the past 25 years, would enable the mine operator to carry the coal at a low figure when he is given his storage certificate; everybody would be assured, for one year, of his coal requirements of the quality he desires. The equity certificate could be used at the banks for further loans, or sold.

E. It would simplify matters very much if gold were denied coinage in U. S. coins. (We do not use gold coin, and foreigners prefer bars). The Mint might deliver gold bars in metric measurements of different sizes, and this gold could be warehoused; fifty per cent Federal Reserve currency being loaned on its value as determined over the 25-year period. Silver could be treated the same way, all our foreign trade balances being paid, if required, by using this particular commodity in bar form.

A person needing the gold for shipment could buy a vault certificate for, say 10 kilos of gold bars, present this, together with Federal Reserve notes obtained from the original loan and would obtain the gold. If a person wanted to ship 10,000 bushels of No. 2 wheat he could buy the equity certificate on the Produce Exchange and presenting it, together with currency or certified check, could order the warehouse to ship the wheat. He would know that the wheat was of the grade called for by the certificate.

F. In this system the requirements of currency would be very great and rather sudden in the case of the cereals as they ripen from Texas to North Dakota and the requirements would be exactly met. The contraction would be fairly slow, being spread over the crop-year; but it would contract exactly in quantity as it expanded; so it is not likely there would be any disturbance in the expansion and contraction of money in this connection. On the other hand, it meets one of the conditions of a good currency. As to currency representing an oversale of credit, that is another matter, far more complex and not within my present study.

G. The reason for having the actual physical operation of these warehouses accomplished by private contractors is to attain a higher efficiency and lower costs than is possible by the use of Government employees, and for other good and sufficient reasons known to business men.

H. The advantage to the farmer of the warehouse system is that while his neighbor the gold miner can bring in his commodity and get full value, any attempt of the farmer to attain parity is met by a glut and a lowering of the price of his commodity which is equal if not superior in value. With this system the farmer's necessities are relieved by effecting a loan for half the value of his commodity; so he can market evenly over longer periods, and probably get a higher price. All these advantages he gets without having to pay interest on half of his product. His neighbor the gold miner pays no interest, and why should not the farmer be relieved, at least partially, in this respect?
Another advantage of the farmer, which is more true with the miner, is that he gets his wheat graded and receives the residue, which I am told is of value, and he gets this at nearly cost. His grading being done by the Government, is prime and the split is finer grading than now in vogue. I am also told by the farmers that there are various practices in vogue whereby the grading, etc., is used for profit by others, causing suspicion and irritation.

I. With our present customs it is probable that speculators perform a very useful function in giving stability to manufacturing by permitting them to enter into future contracts with a guaranteed cost of their raw material. But this is no reason why speculators should be unduly paid for their services and risks as it nearly all comes out of the farmer in the end if he wants

11

to market through them. By this plan the farmer will receive several cents more per bushel than he gets now. His carrying charges will be small.

The country will have just as good a basis for its currency as it now has on commercial credits and possibly in the future, when the world's business enormously increases, this basis will displace gold as backing commodity with countries like France or England, and our proposed system would release more gold commodity for foreign trading. In other words, it may be we could ship Government graded wheat and cotton to pay balances in many cases where we now ship gold bars, which, at times, is undesirable.

J. In normal times our currency is backed by gold to a certain extent. If our people buy an excess of foreign commodities, our gold hoard is diminished and this disturbs the stability of our currency in the minds of many people. It is sometimes serious, as in 1890-1893 when 100 millions of gold were thrown into our hoard by Morgan to save the situation. This allayed apprehension and the panic diminished, but it was rather humiliating for 100 million people to have had such a vulnerable system of money. With other commodities equal or superior in quality to the single gold commodity, this situation is not very likely to occur if we keep a liberal supply of our international commodity in the form of gold bars. The loss of the whole would not raise fears if our internal currency was backed by quick moving commodities at twice their value.

K. There seems to be a considerable misunderstanding among farmers as to the function of a National Bank, conducted strictly on banking principles. They cannot see why those banks cannot loan on farms as security. This is easy to explain. The reason is that most of the money in a bank belongs to the depositors, who, in case of trouble, can demand that it be immediately returned to them. Hence, a National Bank loans at its peril on farms as security. This is a function of a Land Bank, private banker, capitalist, or investor. Loaning money on the actual product of the land is quite a different matter. The Federal Reserve bank permits a National Bank to loan a per cent of its own capital on long term farm mortgages. This does not seem right.

L. The Federal Reserve Bank, in its operation, is copied largely from the Bank of England. It seeks to regulate the volume of money based on credit when credit is oversold, or impaired, and this it does by raising the rate of interest which it will charge the National Banks for lending currency on their commercial paper. This raising the rate of interest is a storm signal not well known to the general public. The higher the rate of interest the more conspicuous the signal. Banks reduce their sales of credit. Some manufacturers diminish their activities, men are discharged, others offer goods at lower prices and glut the market. After a while there is a reduction of currency.

After this goes on for a while then workmen, who do not use banks seemingly, all at once, like a wave, conclude that there is danger of being laid off. Then comes a very conspicuous contraction of the currency. Fifteen million of "Stocking Banks" start doing business. The workman receives as pay, say, $30. Only a few of the bills are of large denomination. He deposits in the "Stocking Bank" the one and two dollar bills, which is all he can spare at a time. Then we have a shortage of small currency. Unfortunately these Stocking Banks keep open for business a long time.

This method of stopping over-loaning (a creation of doubtful credits), if not checked would, in time, lead to a great disaster but the remedy itself is rather severe. In the case of the bank of England it has been generally successful in averting disaster, but twice it failed to work and on another occasion it worked only partially. It seems this method is open to improvement. Improvements in the banking technique and more frequent examinations of discountable paper, together with a continuous discard of doubtful paper offered for rediscount to the Federal Reserve Bank, might be an improvement on the English method of raising the rate of discount.

M. When the amount of credit money passes a certain limit, any extension generally results in impairing its soundness. Prices rise, not in real money, but in impaired money. People do not understand this. The result is extensions and investments and increased production. We attain a fictitious prosperity but a limit is eventually reached. The people who control the money machine become aware that the limit is approaching and that if something is not done to eliminate these excessive impairments of credit there will be a great disaster. They start in to stop the creation of more bad credits and cause liquidation of those already out. Then we have contraction. The value of the currency rises and we have lower prices while the bank optimism is somewhat to blame. Labor with impaired currency of lower buying power strikes for high wages, because the demand for labor rises.

This of itself would not be out of the way but labor forces wages beyond reason, also slacks up and lessons its efforts to produce, and this is as bad as impaired credits. Overproduction takes place, sales slow up, men are discharged, and then, as stated previously, the fifteen million "Stocking Banks" open up and we have still more contraction. The depression is now in full swing.

N. With the warehouse system added to the present Federal Reserve system all our currency will be redeemable either (1) in a gold commodity on demand, or (2) in a mortgaged warehouse commodity CANCELLED on demand. One is as quick as the other, except the delay in handling the more bulky commodity of the warehouse. The warehouse money is produced from the Government loan through its Federal Reserve System on commodities in its own possession and with the margin of safety that is usual with mortgages. In this case it is not obtained by the estimate of an expert whose judgment may err, but by the average of the price actually paid over a period of 25 years, one-half of the value so found being the amount loaned. It can be 40 per cent if thought best, but it should be the same precentage on all articles stored.

O. Generally our currency is based on the principle, normally, that by putting one ounce of gold in a vault you can issue currency calling for two or more ounces on demand. This works, but in the course of the centuries it has failed many times. It would be more scientific to have an ounce of gold back of the currency calling for an ounce. Then when a panic occurred we could issue large amounts of currency and people would accept the extra amount. This is proven by the fact that they do it now. The same currency issued on commodities in warehouses has nearly twice as much value of commodity deposited as is represented by the currency issued.

The advantage of that part of the currency that is issued by the warehouse is: That it does not vary in value; all the capacity for variation in value being transferred to the Deposit Certificate, whereas that part of the currency which is issued on gold varies with the market value of gold bars and through the changeable value of the currency itself. The advantage of the warehouse wealth is that all men can eat most of the stored items and they are not cumulative. The advantage of gold commodity is that it is international and small in bulk and easily transported, and all people accept it.

P. The Warehouse System is to permit the farmer to sell his commodity throughout the crop year and make it unnecessary to dump it on the market all at once. Therefore, the administrative rules will prevent the farmer from speculating by holding his commodity. He must liquidate a portion every month, and cancel his loan to that extent.

Q. Under the present Federal Reserve Bank system the Government furnishes to the banks the printed money upon which they handle trade and perform service and collect fees. These fees are collected under the name of "Interest." The banks themselves also pay interest to their depositors, and require interest on their own Capital Stock. Why should not the Government advance money to its own warehouse system and charge for service performed? The Government stores and the Bankers move notes discounted by a bank on the credit of the merchant and manufacurer, based on a completed barter of actual commodities. This is one of the safest backings of paper money. But the banker is safer when the credit feature is removed and the commodity itself is in a Government Warehouse, graded and obtainable on demand.

In other words, the banker takes no risk, the principal is safe and his profits net, even in a panic. It is quite likely the Government will furnish currency and the Federal Reserve Bank will discount all the notes presented by the banks based on actual commodities in the Government's own possession. The Federal Reserve Bank might even extend its practice of discounting three months notes only, to several months under these conditions.

R. If anything like this plan is favorably received it could be introduced, without any disturbance, by an amendment to the present Federal Reserve Bank Act. Any change whatsoever which affects 100 million people *suddenly* produces great losses until they have rearranged their affairs in line with the change.

S. The history of all the waves of prosperity and depression since the birth of banking systems shows that they have been accentuated by banks loaning to manufacturing and at the same time to agriculture. These are incompatible and no banking system can probably ever be devised that can take care of both simultaneously without these oscillations. Agriculture has one turn-over. Manufacturing has many.

One turn-over (Agriculture) must have long term loans. No banking system can stand that. No system which loans out its deposits, payable on demand, should finance a farmer. It is fatal to stability.

The plan here described will permit the financing of the farmer by his own commodities, the currency issued to him being the common currency of our present Federal Reserve System. This currency at present is payable in gold. When more is issued through the Warehouse System directly by the Government it will still be payable in gold and also redeemable in commodities at fifty per cent of their value. In other words, it is a mortgage on the commodity just as an insurance company loans to the owner of a house and lot fifty per cent of its appraised value, after its value has been appraised. These mortgages are considered the safest of loans.

The Warehouse Loan is even safer. The Government obtains its appraisal by taking the average prices at which the commodities have sold over a period of twenty-five years under the workings of a gold backed system of bank currency—and the result is the average value. It is not the gold; it is the results produced by the workings of a gold based currency for twenty-five years. Once the commodity is appraised, then, like the insurance company, the Government makes a loan of fifty per cent of the appraised value, but, unlike the insurance company, the farmer's loan can be cancelled on demand even the next day. But the limit is one year, and both at the option of the farmer. He no longer needs to glut the market.

16

This plan introduces for the first time a new method of banking, capable of extensive introduction, and assuring absolute security and worth to the Government and to agriculture.
There is no credit or promises introduced. The currency varies in exact proportion as it is needed and it contracts exactly as the commodities move.
Removing these violent changes in demand for currency on account of the season the commercial bank is relieved of these strains and disturbances.

APPENDIX CHARTS:

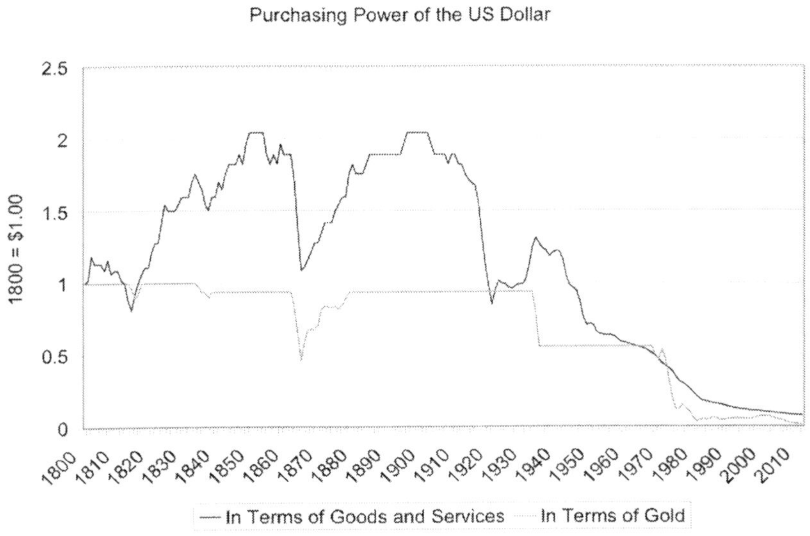

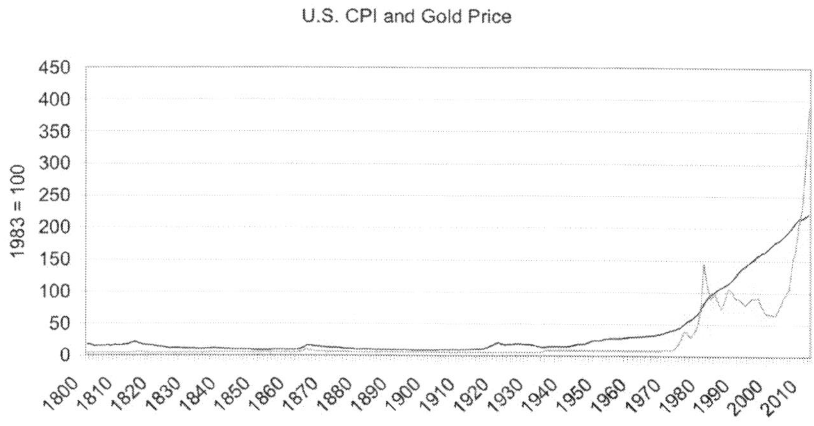

Source: http://www.minneapolisfed.org/community_education/teacher/calc/hist1800.cfm and http://www.finfacts.ie/Private/curency/goldmarketprice.htm

BIBLIOGRAPHY

Ahamed, L., 2009, *Lords of Finance*, London: Penguin Books.

Alston, L.J. 1983. "Farm Foreclosures in the United States during the Interwar Period." *Journal of Economic History*, Vol. 43(4): pps. 885-903.

Alston, L.J. Grove, W.A. and Wheelock, D.C., 1994, *Why Do Banks Fail? Evidence from the 1920s Explorations in Economic History*, October 1994, Vol. 31 (4), pp. 409-31.

Atack, J., and Passell, P., 1994, *A New Economic View of American History*, 2nd ed., New York: W.W. Norton & Company.

Babson, R. to Edison, T.A., March 9, April 1, May 3, Banking 1922, TENHP.

Baldwin, N., 1995, 2001, *Edison: Inventing the Century*, Chicago: Chicago University Press.

Baruch, BM., 1960, *Baruch: The Public Years*, New York: Holt, Rinehart and Winston.

Baruch to Edison, May 26, 1922, Banking 1922, TENHP.

Berridge, W.A.,1922, "Cycles of Employment and Unemployment in the United States, 1914-1921," *The Journal of the American Statistical Association*, Vol. 18, No. 137, pp. 42-53.

Best, G.D., 2003, *Dollar Decade*, Westport, CN: Praeger Publishers.

Blumhart, H.J., Adair, IA, April 5, 1922. TENHP Banking 1922

Bordo, M.D., *The Gold Standard & Related Regimes*, 1999, Cambridge: Cambridge University Press.

Brownson, Sr., E.S., to Edison, March 23, 1922, Banking 1922, TENHP.

Buol, J.J., and Vaughan, M.D., "Rules vs. Discretion—The Wrong Choice Could Open the Floodgates," *The Regional Economist*, Federal Reserve Bank of St. Louis, pps. 10-11, January 2003.

Capper, A., to Edison, June 9, 1923, Banking 1923, TENHP.

Conot, R., 1979, *A Streak of Luck*, New York: Seaview Books.

Dimand, R.W., 2003, "Competing Visions for the U.S. Monetary System, 1907-1913: The Quest for an Elastic Currency and the Rejection of Fisher's Compensated Dollar Rule for Price Stability," *Cahiers d'économie politique*, 45, pp. 101-121.

Dorfman, J., 1949, *The Economic Mind in American Civilization, Vol. Four*, New York: Viking Press.

Dorn, J.A., and Schwartz, A.J., 1983, *The Search for Stable Money-Essays on Monetary Reform*, Chicago: Chicago University Press.

Edison, "A Proposed Amendment to the Federal Reserve Banking System", May 1922., TENHP.

Edison Undated, handwritten, notes in Banking 1922, TENHP.

Edison to Babson, R., April 6, 1922, Banking 1922, TENHP.

Edison to Babson, R., April 8, 1922, Banking 1922, TENHP.

Edison to Babson, R., May 1, 1922, Banking 1922, TENHP.

Edison to Baruch, B., May 29, 1922, Banking 1922, TENHP.

Edison to C.P Bump, West-Logan Farmers Union, Clay Co., NB, April 27, 1922; Banking 1922, TENHP.

Edison to Capper, A., July 31, 1922. Banking 1922, TENHP.

Edison to Edmonds, R.H., Editor, *Manufacturers Record*, Wenersville, PA, July 24, 1922. TENHP Banking 1922.

Edison to Fisher, I., August 7, 1922; Banking 1922

Edison to Fisher, I., December 19, 1922.

Edison to Goss, A.S., Washington State Grange, Seattle, WA, December 21, 1922.

Edison to Graham, M.K., April 30, 1924. Banking 1924, TENHP.

Edison to Graham, M.K., Graham, TX, April 20, 1922. All letters in Banking 1922, TENHP.

Edison to Harding, W.P.G., February 21, 1922. Banking 1922. TENHP.

Edison to Pierre Jay (New York Federal Reserve Bank), April 1922, in Banking, TENHP.

Edison to Johnston, W.B., Kansas City, MO, July 24, 1922, Banking 1922, TENHP.

Edison to Johnston, W.B., Kansas City, MO, July 27, 1922, Banking 1922, TENHP.

Edison to Joyce, T., Washington, D.C., July 24, 1922, Banking 1922, TENHP.

Edison to Ludlow, I., New York City, April 24, 1922.

Edison to McDermott, G.T., Topeka, KS, April 26, 1922.

Edison to President of University of Wisconsin, March 3, Banking 1922.

Edison, Proposal "Revise May 13, 1922" is in Banking 1922, TENHP.

Edison to Rings, A.W., Mayetta, KS, April 20, 1922, Banking 1922.

Edison to Rings, A.W., May 9, 1922. TENHP Banking 1922.

Edison to Roberts, G., V.P., National City Bank, New York City, March 14, 1922; both letters in Banking 1922, TENHP.

Edison to Sanford, H.W., Knoxville, TN, March 8, 1922, Banking 1922, TENHP.

Edison to *Topeka Capital,* Editor, Topeka, KS, April 12, 1922. Banking 1922, TENHP.

Edison to Wannamaker, J.S., May 5 and 6, Banking 1922, TENHP.

Edison to Willis, February 2, Banking 1922, TENHP.

Edison to Wannamaker, J.S., May 12, 1922. TENHP Banking 1922.

Ferrell, Robert H. (ed.), 2010, *Inside the Nixon Administration-The Secret Diary of Arthur Burns*, 1969-1974, University Press of Kansas, Lawrence, KS.

Fischer, D.H., 1996, *The Great Wave,* New York: Oxford University Press.

Fisher, I., 1911, 1922, *The Purchasing Power of Money*. New York: The Macmillan Company.

Fisher, I., 1934, *Stable Money*, New York: Adelphi Company.

Fisher, I., 1920, *Stabilizing the Dollar*, New York: The Macmillan Company.

Fisher, I. to Edison, July 31, Banking 1922.

Fisher, I., to Edison, August 11, 1922, Banking 1922,

Foster, W.T., and Catchings, W., *Saturday Evening Post,* December 23, 1922.

Foster, W.T., Catchings, W., "Edison-Ford Commodity Money," address before the annual meeting of the American Academy of Political Science, November 23, 1922.

Foster, W.T., and Catchings, W., 1924, *Money, 2nd ed.*, Boston and New York: Houghton Mifflin Publishing.

FRB-Minneapolis:
http://www.minneapolisfed.org/community_education/teacher/calc/hist1800.cfm

Frieden, J., 1996, "Economic Integration and the Politics of Monetary Policy in the United States," pps. 108-136, in *Internationalization and Domestic Politics*, ed. Robert Keohane and Helen Milner, 1996, Cambridge: Cambridge University Press.

Frieden, J., 1997, *Monetary Populism in Nineteenth-Century America: An Open Economy Interpretation, Journal of Economic History, Vol. 57, No. 2*, pps. 367-392.

Friedman, Milton, 1960, *A Program for Monetary Stability*, New York: Fordham University Press.

Friedman, M., and Schwartz, A.J., 1963, *A Monetary History of the United States, 1867-1960*, Princeton: Princeton University Press.

Garrett, G., *Where the Money Grows*, 1911, New York: Harper and Brothers.

Grandin, Greg, 2009, *Fordlandia: The Rise and Fall of Henry Ford's Forgotten Jungle City*, Picador, New York, Henry Holt and Co.

Hammes, D.L., 2001, "Locating the Federal Reserve Districts and Headquarters Cities", September 2001, Vol. 15, No. 3, *The Region*, the quarterly journal of the Minneapolis Federal Reserve Bank, ISSN 1045-3369, pps. 24-27, and 55-65.

Hammes, D.L., and Wills, D.T., 2004, "Edison's Plan to Reinvent Money," *Financial History*, Winter. No. 80, pps. 16-20, ISSN 1520-4723.

Hammes, D. L., and Wills, D.T., 2005a, "Black Gold: The End of Bretton Woods and the Oil Price Shocks of the 1970s", in *The Independent Review*, Vol. 9, No.4, Spring 2005, ISSN 1086-1653.

Hammes, D.L., and Wills, D.T., 2005b, "Thomas Edison's 'Except One": The Monetary Views of Arthur Kitson Revisited," in *The Journal of Economic Studies*, Vol. 32, No. 1, ISSN 0144-3585.

Hammes, D.L., and Wills, D.T., 2006, "Thomas Edison's Monetary Option" in *The Journal of the History of Economic Thought.* (Vol. 28, No. 3, September 2006). ISSN 1042-7716., pps. 295-308.

Hansen, J.M., 1991, *Gaining Access: Congress and the Farm Lobby, 1919-1981*, Chicago: The University of Chicago Press.

Harding, W.P.G., speech, "Credit, Currency and Business" was addressed to the Southern Wholesale Dry Goods Association, Birmingham, AL, May 10, 1922. Copy in Banking 1922, TENHP

Harding, W.P.G., 1925, *The Formative Period of the Federal Reserve System*, New York: Houghton Mifflin. pps. 222, 238-245.

Hawley, E.W.(ed.), 1982, *Herbert Hoover as Secretary of Commerce: Studies in New Era Thought and Practice*, Hoover Presidential Library Association, Ames: University of Iowa Press.

Hazlitt , H., 1921, December 9, 1921, *The New York Evening Mail.*

Herman, M.B., St. Paul, MN, to Edison, September 10, 1922. in Banking, 1922, TENHP.

Hicks, J.D., 1928, "The Sub-Treasury: A Forgotten Plan for the Relief of Agriculture," *The Mississippi Valley Historical Review*, 15 (3), pp. 355-373.

Hicks, J.D., *The Populist Revolt: A History of the Farmers' Alliance and the People's Party*, Lincoln: University of Nebraska Press, 1961 [c1959].

Hoover to Capper, July 19, 1922, Banking 1922, TENHP.

Humphrey, T.M., "The Real Bills Doctrine," *The Economic Review*, The Federal Reserve Bank of Richmond, September/October 1982, pps.3-12.

Im, E.I., Hammes, D.L., and Wills, D.T., 2006, "Stationarity Condition for AR Index Process", in *Econometric Theory*, Vol. 22, No.1, pp. 164-168, February 2006.

Israel, P., 1998, *Edison: A Life of Invention*, New York: John Wiley & Sons, Inc.

Josephson, M., 1959, *Edison: A Biography*, New York: History Book Club.

Keynes, J.M., 1923, *A Tract on Monetary Reform*, London: The Macmillan Press, Ltd.

Kindleberger, C.P., 1989. *Manias, Panics, and Crashes: A History of Financial Crises (Wiley Investment Classics)*, 2nd ed., Hoboken: J.W. Wiley and Sons.

Kitson, A., to Edison, March 3, 1922, Banking 1922.

Kyvig, D.E., 2004, *Daily Life in the United States, 1920-1940*. Chicago: Ivan Dee Publishing.

Lacey, R., *Ford*, Boston: Little, Brown and Company.

"List of names to whom Money Questionnaires have been sent", undated, Banking 1922, TENHP.

Ludlow, I., Ludlow Syndicate, New York City, to Edison, April 17, 1922;

Mayhew, 1972, "A Reappraisal of the Causes of Farm Protest in he United States, 1870-1900," *The Journal of Economic History*, Vol. 34 (2): 464–475.

Meadowcroft, F.R., to Babson, Banking 1922, TENHP. (April 12?)

Mehrling, P.G., 2002, "Economists and the Fed: Beginnings," *Journal of Economic Perspectives*, 16 (4), pp. 207-217.

Mehrling, P.G., 1997, *The Money Interest and the Public Interest*, Cambridge: Harvard University Press.

Meltzer, A.H., 2003, *A History of the Federal Reserve: Vol.1: 1913-1951*. Chicago: Chicago University Press.

Miller, N., 2003, *New World Coming*, Da Capo Press.

Moen, J. (2001), "John Law and the Mississippi Bubble: 1718-1720." *Mississippi History Now*, at: http://mshistory.k12.ms.us/articles/70/john-law-and-the-mississippi-bubble-1718-1720; accessed May 30, 2010.

Mowry, D.E., General Secretary, Madison Association of Commerce. Letter to Edison March 23, 1922, Banking 1922. TENHP.

Muscle Shoals: "The History of the City of Muscle Shoals", http://www.cityofmuscleshoals.com/Default.asp?ID=11;

"National Leader", to Edison February 21, 1922. Banking 1922. TENHP.

New York Times, February 12, 1914, page 1.

New York Times, August 23, 1921, page 31.

New York Times, December 6, 1921, page 6.

New York Times, Dec.15, 1921, page 26.

New York Times, July 16, 1922, page E5, Section Seven, pages 1 and 2.

New York Times, July 18, 1922, page 27.

New York Times, July 23, 1922, page 34, 84, 91.

Odell, K.A., and Weidenmier, M.D., 2004, "Real Shock, Monetary Aftershock: The 1906 San Francisco Earthquake and the Panic of 1907," *The Journal of Economic History*, Vol. 64, No.4, pps. 1002-1027.

Panton, S.P., to Edison, January 17, 1922, Banking 1922, TENHP.

Price, T., Editor, *Commerce and Finance*, New York City, to Edison, May 29, 1922; Banking 1922, TENHP.

Rings, A.W., Mayetta, KS, to Thomas Edison, April 26, 1922.

Rockoff, H., http://eh.net/encyclopedia/article/Rockoff.WWI

Rolnick, A.J., and Weber, W.E., 1997, "Money, Inflation, and Output under Fiat and Commodity Standards," *The Journal of Political Economy*, Vol. 105, No. 6, pps. 1308-1321.

Romer, C., 1999, "Changes in Business Cycles: Evidence and Explanations," *The Journal of Economic Perspectives*, Vol. 13, No. 2, Spring, pps. 23-44.

Santayana, G., *Life of Reason, Reason in Common Sense*, Scribner's, 1905.

Scott to Edison, Feb 27 and March 14, Banking 1922. TENHP.

Skidelsky, R., *John Maynard Keynes: Vol. 2, The Economist As Saviour*, 1920-1937, New York: The Penguin Press.

Smiley, G., "The U.S. Economy in the 1920s", http://eh.net/encyclopedia/article/smiley.1920s.final

Smithsonian Folkways, 2007, CD *If You Ain't Got the Do-Re-Mi: Songs of Rags and Riches.* http://media.smithsonianfolkways.org/liner_notes/smithsonian_folkways/SFW40195.pdf, viewed December 31, 2011.

US Census: http://www.census.gov/population/censusdata/urpop0090.txt

U.S. Department of Commerce, Bureau of the Census, Historical Statistics of the United States, Colonial Times to 1970, Part 1, Washington, D.C.

U.S. Department of Commerce, Bureau of the Census, Brissenden, Paul, 'Earnings of Factory Workers, 1899 to 1927, ' Washington, U.S. GPO, 1929.

U.S. Government Printing Office, "Report of the President's Conference on Unemployment," Washington, GPO, 1921.

Van Lear, W., "A Review of the Rules versus Discretion Debate in Monetary Policy," *Eastern Economic Journal*, Vol. 26, No.1, Winter 2000, pp. 29-39.

Vedder, R.K., and Gallaway, L.E., 1993, *Out of Work*, New York: Holmes & Meier Publishers, Inc.

Vrooman, W.L., to Edison, April 6, 1922. TENHP Banking 1922.

Walter, J.R., "Depression-Era Bank Failures: The Great Contagion or the Great Shakeout?" *Economic Quarterly*, FRB Richmond, Vol. 91/1 Winter 2005.

Wanamaker, J.S., to Edison, April 29, May 1, 20, 1922. All in TENHP, Banking 1922.

Warburg to Edison, Banking 1922.

Weston to Edison, Banking 1922.

White, A.D., 1896, 1933, *Fiat Money Inflation In France.* New York: Appleton-Century Company.

Wikipedia: http://en.wikipedia.org/wiki/Charles_E._Mitchell, accessed January 4, 2012.

Willis to Edison. February 6 and 24, 1922. Banking 1922. TENHP.

Wood, C.F., V.P., Warrant Export & Discount Corporation, Birmingham, AL, to Edison, dated July 20, 1922, Banking 1922, TENHP.

INDEX

["n"=footnote reference]

ABOUT THE AUTHOR

David L. Hammes has taught economics at universities in Canada, Australia, and the United States since the early 1970s. He has been in the economics department at the University of Hawaii at Hilo since 1988. Hammes' writings on economic topics, including the early history of the Federal Reserve System, have appeared in many academic journals in the field. His earlier book, *Shaping Our Nation*, was published in 1988. Hammes lives in Hilo, Hawaii, with his wife Kathy. They have two grown sons, Mark and Steven, living in California. Contact David at hammes@hawaii.edu.

16342793R00088

Made in the USA
Lexington, KY
20 July 2012